ILLUSTRATED WILDLIFE ENCYCLOPEDIA

LARGE MAMMALS

This edition published by Lorenz Books

Lorenz Books is an imprint of
Anness Publishing Ltd
Hermes House, 88–89 Blackfriars Road
London SE1 8HA
tel. 020 7401 2077; fax 020 7633 9499
www.lorenzbooks.com; info@anness.com

© Anness Publishing Ltd 2000, 2003

This edition distributed in the UK by
Aurum Press Ltd, 25 Bedford Avenue,
London WC1B 3AT
tel. 020 7637 3225; fax 020 7580 2469

This edition distributed in the USA and
Canada by National Book Network
4720 Boston Way, Lanham, MD 20706
tel. 301 459 3366; fax 301 459 1705
www.nbnbooks.com
customer.service@macmillan.com.au

This edition distributed in New Zealand
by David Bateman Ltd, 30 Tarndale
Grove, Off Bush Road, Albany, Auckland
tel. (09) 415 7664; fax (09) 415 8892

This edition distributed in Australia by
Pan Macmillan Australia,
Level 18, St Martins Tower, 31 Market St
Sydney, NSW 2000
tel. 1300 135 113; fax 1300 135 103

A CIP catalogue record for this book is
available from the British Library.

Publisher: Joanna Lorenz
Managing Editor, Children's Books:
  Gilly Cameron Cooper
Senior Editor: Nicole Pearson
Editors: Simon Beecroft, Nicky
  Barber, Charlotte Hurdman,
  Louisa Somerville
Designers: Vivienne Gordon, Mirjana
  Nociar, Caroline Reeves, Traffika,
  Simon Wilder, Sarah Williams
Picture Researchers: Kay Rowley,
  Adrian Bentley, Cathy Stastny,
  Elizabeth Walsh
Illustrators: Julian Baker, Peter Bull,
  Vanessa Card, David Webb
Production Controller: Ann Childers
Editorial Reader: Jonathan Marshall

Previously published as *Big Mammals*

10 9 8 7 6 5 4 3 2 1

ILLUSTRATED WILDLIFE ENCYCLOPEDIA

LARGE MAMMALS

Discover how Nature's most
impressive animals live and
survive in the wild

TAYLOR, KLEVANSKY, BRIGHT, KERROD

LORENZ BOOKS

C O N T

E N T S

BEARS AND PANDAS 128

WHALES AND DOLPHINS 188

Introducing Mammals

The elephants, big cats, bears and whales featured in this book have one thing in common – they are all mammals. This means that, like us, they are warm-blooded and the mothers suckle their young with milk. The 5,000 or so species of mammal in existence today all evolved from tiny, shrew-like animals that lived some 80 million years ago. This book looks at many kinds of mammal, both on land and in the sea, from carnivores, such as lions, to herbivores, such as elephants. You will also learn something of their extinct relatives, such as the woolly mammoth. Find out about the ways in which people have harnessed mammals, and now threaten some of them with extinction. This book shows us the beauty of mammals and reminds us that their future is in our hands.

One Big Family

Scientists have tried to work out the origins and relationships between the different groups of mammals for many years. It is thought that Megazostrodon (shown at the top of this chart) is the most likely common ancestor of the mammals in existence today. The chart below shows one possible way that mammals may have evolved.

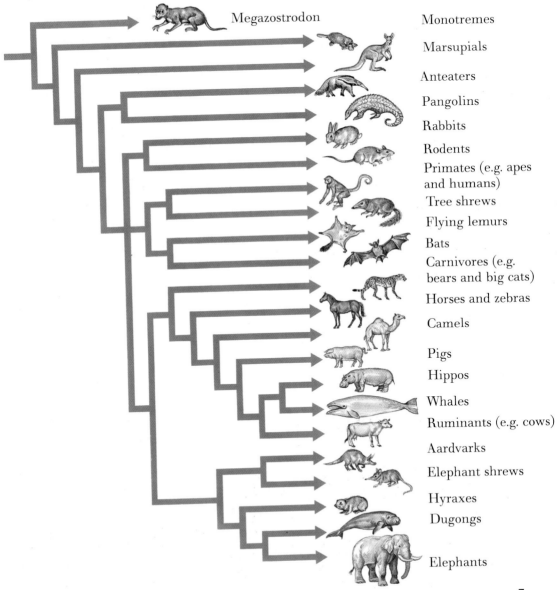

Megazostrodon

Monotremes

Marsupials

Anteaters

Pangolins

Rabbits

Rodents

Primates (e.g. apes and humans)

Tree shrews

Flying lemurs

Bats

Carnivores (e.g. bears and big cats)

Horses and zebras

Camels

Pigs

Hippos

Whales

Ruminants (e.g. cows)

Aardvarks

Elephant shrews

Hyraxes

Dugongs

Elephants

Elephants

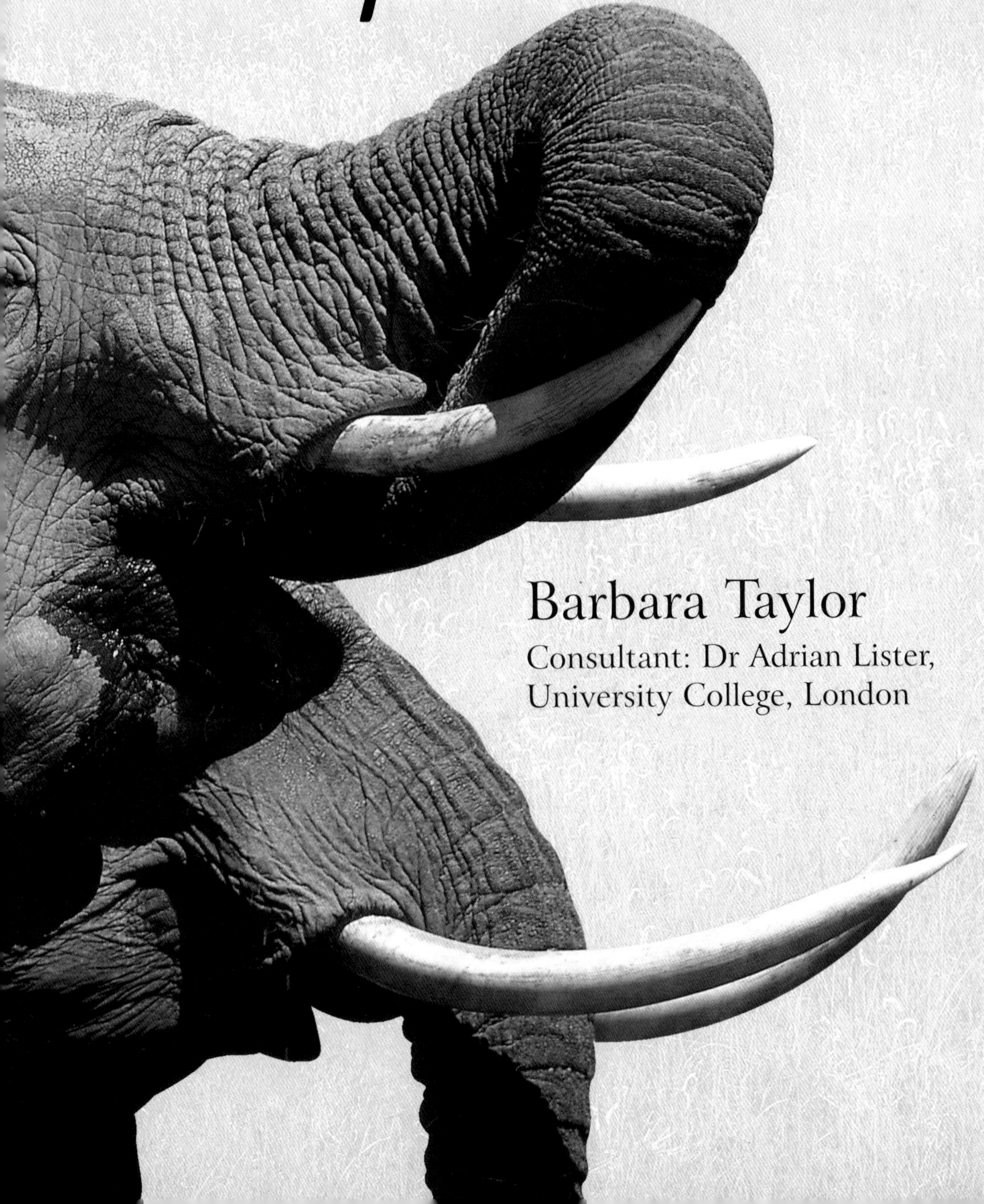

Barbara Taylor
Consultant: Dr Adrian Lister,
University College, London

What is an Elephant?

Elephants are the largest and heaviest creatures on land. An African male (bull) elephant weighs as much as 80 people, 6 cars, 12 large horses or 1,500 cats! Elephants are extremely strong and can pick up whole trees with their trunks. They are also highly intelligent, gentle animals. Females live together in family groups and look after one another. Like human beings, elephants are mammals. As with all mammals, they can control their body temperature and, like most mammals, they give birth to babies. After humans, elephants are the longest lived of all mammals. Some live to be about 70 years old. Two species of elephant exist today – the African elephant and the Asian elephant. Both have a trunk, large ears and thick, grey skin. Not all elephants have tusks, however. Generally, only African elephants and male Asian elephants have tusks.

▲ **WORKING ELEPHANTS**
In India, domesticated (tamed) elephants are used by farmers to carry heavy loads. In some Asian countries they also move heavy logs by pulling them.

Indra and the Elephant
One of the most celebrated Hindu gods, Indra, rides a mighty white elephant called Airavata. In Hinduism (the main religion of India), elephants are sacred animals. One of Indra's emblems is the ankus, a special pointed stick used to control elephants. Indra is shown holding an ankus in this painting.

Tail, with a brush of thick hair at the end.

▼ UNUSUAL FEATURES

The mighty elephant is a record-breaking beast. Not only is it the largest land animal, it is also the second tallest (only the giraffe is taller). It has larger ears, teeth and tusks than any other animal. The elephant is also one of the few animals to have a nose in the form of a long trunk.

The huge ear of an African elephant.

FAMILY LIFE ▲

Adult male and female elephants do not live together in family groups. Instead, adult sisters and daughters live in groups led by an older female. Adult males (bulls) live on their own or in all-male groups.

Small eyes, protected by long eyelashes.

Wrinkly skin with hardly any hair.

Long trunk, used as a nose and an extra hand.

Gently curved tusks, used for digging, fighting and lifting.

Strong legs and flat feet for support.

BABY ELEPHANTS ▲

An elephant baby feels safe between its mother's front legs. It spends most of the first year of its life there. Mother elephants look after their young for longer than any other animal parent except humans. Daughters never leave the family group unless the group becomes too big.

11

African or Asian?

How do you tell an African elephant from an Asian elephant? They seem alike, but they are not identical. The most obvious difference is in the size of the ears — the African elephant's are larger. In Africa, too, elephants have longer legs and a more slender body than their Asian relatives. The back of the Asian elephant is arched, while the African species has a dip in its back. Another difference is tusks — in Asia usually only males have visible tusks, whereas in Africa both male and female elephants normally have them.

▲ AFRICAN SHAPE

You can always tell an African elephant from its large ears and the dip in its back. This species of elephant usually holds its head slightly lower than its shoulders. The male African elephant stands on average 3.3m at the shoulder, while females are about 2.8m tall. The male weighs about 5,000kg (5 tonnes), which is about the same weight as a truck.

▶ CONTINENTAL EARS

Some people say that the large, triangular ears of the African elephant (*right*) are shaped like the continent of Africa, while the ears of an Asian elephant are shaped like India. In fact, ears are like fingerprints — they are different on each individual. Scientists look closely at the pattern of veins, notches and tears on the ears to identify individual elephants.

▶ HEAD UP

The Latin name of the Asian elephant, *Elephas maximus*, means huge arch. This refers to the upturned shape of its back. The Asian elephant usually holds its head above its body, so that the top of its head is the highest point of the body.

▲ ASIAN TUSKS

The tusks of a male Asian elephant are shorter and lighter than those of an African elephant. Female Asian elephants have very small tusks or none at all.

Did you know? The heaviest known African elephant weighed 7 tonnes.

▼ SKIN SPOTS

Elephants are usually thought of as grey. However, some Asian elephants have pink patches of skin. These patches are commonly found on the ears, trunk and face. They generally develop as the animal grows older. African elephants rarely have them.

▲ THE HAIRY ONE

Asian elephants have more hair than their African relatives, and baby Asian elephants (*above*) are hairier still. As baby elephants grow up, most of this protective hair is worn away.

Elephant Habitats

The two main species of elephant are divided into smaller groups called subspecies. These subspecies each look a little different from one another and are named after their habitats. Africa has three subspecies – the bush elephant of the open grasslands, the forest elephant of west and central Africa, and the desert elephant of Namibia. The main subspecies in Asia is the Indian and southeast Asian elephant. Asia is also home to the Sri Lankan elephant and the Sumatran elephant, which lives on the islands of Sumatra and Borneo (parts of Indonesia).

▲ **SUMATRAN ELEPHANT**
These elephants wade into swamps to find juicy grasses to feast on. They are the smallest of the three Asian subspecies. Sumatran elephants are also the lightest in colour, and they have fewer pink patches than the other Asian subspecies.

SRI LANKAN ELEPHANT ▶
The rare Sri Lankan elephant is the biggest and darkest of the three Asian subspecies. Many of the 2,500 – 2,700 elephants in Sri Lanka live in protected national parks or nature reserves.

Did you know? The desert elephant is the tallest elephant in the world, at up to 4.21 m high.

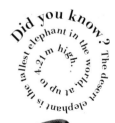

◀ **FOREST ELEPHANTS**
The forest elephant (*Loxodonta africana cyclotis*) is the smallest African subspecies. Its size enables it to move easily through the trees. Generally, its ears are small and rounded, and its tusks are less curved than those of other African elephants.

◀ DESERT ELEPHANTS

The hot, dry deserts of Namibia in southwest Africa are home to the rare desert elephant. This subspecies is very closely related to the African bush elephant, but it has longer legs. Desert elephants have to walk long distances to find food and water. Scientists think that this is why they have longer legs than any other subspecies.

▶ ELEPHANT WORLD

African elephants live in a scattered band across central and southern Africa. They became extinct in North Africa around AD300. Today, Asian elephants live in hilly or mountainous areas of India, Sri Lanka, southeast Asia, Malaysia, Indonesia and southern China. In the past, they roamed right across Asia.

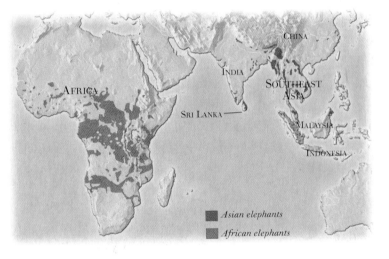

Asian elephants
African elephants

▲ BUSH ELEPHANTS

African bush elephants live in savanna (areas of grassland with scattered trees). However, some live in forests or marshes and even on mountains.

◀ SOLIDLY BUILT

The African bush elephant, *Loxodonta africana africana*, is bulkier and heavier than any other elephant subspecies. Like all elephants, its large size is a useful weapon against lions, tigers and other predators.

Big Bones

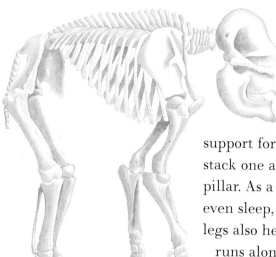

An elephant's legs are placed directly underneath its body, like a table's legs. This arrangement provides a firm support for its great weight. The leg bones stack one above the other to form a strong, tall pillar. As a result, an elephant can rest, and even sleep, while standing up. The pillar-like legs also help to hold up the backbone, which runs along the top of the animal and supports the ribs. The backbones of both African and Asian elephants arch upwards in the middle. Their differently shaped backs are produced by bony spines that stick up from the backbone. The elephant's skeleton is not just built for strength, however. It is also flexible enough to let the elephant kneel and squat easily.

▲ BONY BACK

Long spines stick up from the backbone of the Asian elephant's skeleton. The muscles that hold up the head are joined to these spines and to the back of the skull.

Young male Asian elephant's skull

Large eye hole.

Start of tusk.

▲ CAGED IN

The skull is the bony box that protects the brain and holds the huge teeth and tusks. The skull above is that of a young elephant with undeveloped tusks. On an adult male the upper jaw juts out further than the lower jaw because it contains the roots for the heavy tusks.

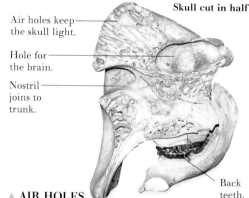

Skull cut in half

Air holes keep the skull light.

Hole for the brain.

Nostril joins to trunk.

Back teeth.

▲ AIR HOLES

An elephant has a large skull compared to the size of its body. However, a honeycomb of air holes inside the skull makes it lighter than it looks from the outside.

Long, curved tusks.

Huge backbone and rib cage.

◄ **MAMMOTH SKELETON**

In 1799, an incredible discovery was made in Siberia. The preserved skeleton of a woolly mammoth was found buried in the ice. Mammoths are prehistoric relatives of the elephant. They died out about 10,000 years ago. Mammoths were a similar size to elephants today, with longer tusks.

Sometimes the contents of the stomach are preserved along with the bones.

General Hannibal
In 218BC, the famous North African general Hannibal planned to attack the Roman army – using elephants. The elephants were led over the Alps (a mountain range in Europe) and taken across rivers by raft. Sadly, most of them died and Hannibal had to admit defeat.

Hole for eye.

Rounded forehead of male African elephant.

Curved ribs.

Trunk opening.

▶ **AFRICAN SKELETON**

The African elephant's forehead is smooth and rounded, whereas an Asian's skull and head have two domes on top. The large hole in the skull is the trunk opening, and the tusks fit into the skull from the upper jaw.

Powerful leg bones.

These record-breaking tusks measure 2.85m (*left*) and 2.97m (*right*).

17

Tusks

An elephant's tusks are its front teeth. The part that we see is just two-thirds of the tusk's total length. The rest is hidden in the skull. Tusks are made from a very hard material called ivory. Elephants mainly use their tusks for feeding. The sharp ends are ideal for digging up edible roots and stripping bark from trees. Tusks are also used as weapons, and help to protect the trunk, like a car bumper. Elephants are born with milk tusks, which are replaced by permanent tusks when the elephant is between 6-12 months old. They grow continuously at the rate of about 17cm a year. As the tip wears down, more tusk is pushed out from the skull.

▲ TINY TUSKS

Some female Asian elephants have small tusks called tushes. They grow so slowly that they hardly stick out of the mouth. Some male Asian elephants have no tusks.

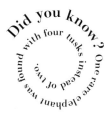

This elephant's left-hand tusk is shorter than the right-hand one because it has been used more.

Male elephant tusks weigh up to 60kg, or about the weight of two children. Female tusks are lighter and weigh 9kg on average.

Did you know? One rare elephant was found with four tusks instead of two.

◀ TUSK SHAPES

Elephants tend to be either right-handed or left-handed, just as human beings are. Their tusks are like hands and elephants prefer to use one of them more than the other one. As a result, the favourite one becomes more worn. Tusks also come in different shapes and sizes. Some are slim and straight, while others stick out at different angles or even cross in front.

◀ USEFUL TUSKS

African elephants dig for salt with their tusks. They loosen the soil with the sharp points, just as we use a garden fork. On occasions, elephants also dig for salt in caves under the ground.

▼ MAMMOTH TUSKS

The tusks of extinct mammoths could be 2.5-3m long – half as long again as the tusks of most African elephants today. Mammoth tusks tended to curve first outwards and then inwards, although the female's tusks were more symmetrical and smaller than the male's. Early humans hunted mammoths for food. They also built huts from the bones.

African bull (male) tusk

African cow (female) tusk

Asian bull (male) tusk

▲ FIGHTING ELEPHANTS

In ancient India, humans trained elephants to help them fight battles. The elephant's sharp tusks were deadly when used as weapons. In ancient Rome, elephants were made to battle against gladiators (trained fighters) and other animals for sport. Cruelly, the elephants were usually forced to fight against their own gentle nature.

◀ RAW MATERIALS

Tusks are made of solid ivory, which is a type of dentine. This is a hard material that forms the main part of all mammal teeth. Nerves and blood vessels run through the tusks. The blood carries food to feed the growing tusk. Elephants feel pain and pressure in their tusks, just as we can in our teeth.

19

Body Parts

An elephant's skin is thick, grey and wrinkly, and surprisingly sensitive. Some insects, including flies and mosquitoes, can bite into it. Often, elephants roll around in the mud to keep flies from biting them (as well as cooling the elephant down). Underneath the skin, the elephant has typical mammal body parts, only much larger. The heart, for example, is about five times bigger than a human heart and weighs up to 21kg – the weight of a small child. Also, an elephant's huge intestines can weigh nearly a tonne, including the contents. The powerful lungs are operated by strong muscles. These let the elephant breathe underwater whilst using its trunk as a snorkel.

▲ **THICK SKIN**
An elephant's skin is 2.5cm thick on the back and in some areas of the head. But in other places, such as around the mouth, the skin is paper thin.

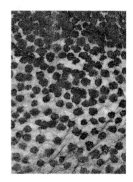

▲ **PINK SKIN**
An elephant gets its colour from dots of grey pigment (colouring) in the skin. As it ages, this grey pigment may gradually fade so that the skin looks pink.

Did you know? Some very rare Asian elephants have a white skin.

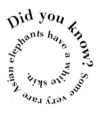

◀ **ELEPHANT HAIR**
The hairiest part of an elephant is the end of its tail. The tail hairs are many times thicker than human hair and grow into thick tufts. Apart from the end of the tail, the chin and around the eyes and ears, the elephant is not a particularly hairy animal.

▲ PINK TRUNKS

Some Asian elephants, particularly the Sri Lankan subspecies, have pink trunks. They may also have pink patches on their ears, face and belly, which are a sign of ageing. This is comparable to the human hair turning grey.

Flying Elephants

According to an Indian folk tale, elephants could once fly. This ability was taken away by a hermit with magical powers when a flock of elephants woke him from a deep trance. The elephants landed in a tree above him, making a lot of noise and causing a branch to fall on his head. The hermit was so furious that he cast a magical spell.

▼ INSIDE AN ELEPHANT

If you could look inside the body of an elephant, you would see its huge skeleton supporting the inner organs. The elephant cross-section shown here is of a female elephant.

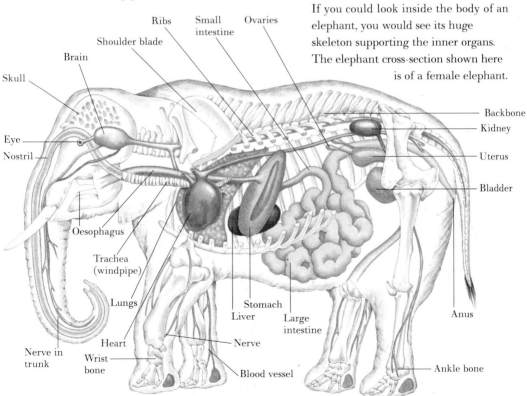

Labels: Ribs, Small intestine, Ovaries, Shoulder blade, Brain, Skull, Eye, Nostril, Backbone, Kidney, Uterus, Bladder, Oesophagus, Trachea (windpipe), Lungs, Stomach, Liver, Large intestine, Anus, Nerve, Heart, Nerve in trunk, Wrist bone, Blood vessel, Ankle bone

Elephant Senses

Elephants use the five senses to learn about their surroundings – hearing, sight, smell, touch and taste. The most important sense is smell, which they rely on more than any other. Elephants smell through the trunk, using it as a directional nose. The trunk is also particularly sensitive to touch and has short hairs that help the elephant feel things. The tip of the trunk is used to investigate food, water and other objects. It can tell whether something is hot, cold, sharp or smooth. Elephants communicate with each other largely by sound. They make rumbling sounds, most of which are too low for humans to hear. Touch is also crucial for communication. When two elephants meet, each places the tip of its trunk in the other's mouth as a greeting.

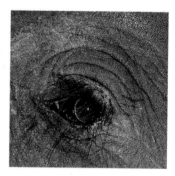

▲ **ELEPHANT EYES**
All elephants' eyes are brown with long lashes. They are small in relation to the huge head. Elephants are colour blind and do not see well in direct, strong sunlight. Their eyesight is better in darker, forest conditions.

Did you know? An African elephant's ear is as big as a single bed sheet and can weigh as much as a person.

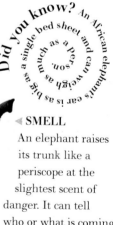

◄ **SMELL**
An elephant raises its trunk like a periscope at the slightest scent of danger. It can tell who or what is coming towards it just from the smells picked up by the sensitive trunk. The sense of smell is so powerful that an elephant can pick up the scent of a human being from more than 1.5km away.

◄ USING EARS

An elephant strains to hear a distant noise by putting its ears forward to catch the sound. It also does this when it is curious about a certain noise. Elephants have a well developed sense of hearing. Their enormous ears pick up the rumble of other elephants from up to about 8km away. Male elephants also flap their ears to spread a special scent that lets other elephants know they are there.

◄ HEARING RANGE

Elephants can hear low sounds called infrasound. Human beings cannot hear infrasound although we can sometimes feel it. Some animals, such as bats and mice, can hear very high sounds called ultrasound.

ULTRASOUND

bats
porpoises insects shrews
birds
crocodilians
humans
dogs
fin and blue whale
elephants

Frequency (hertz)
18,000
50

INFRASOUND

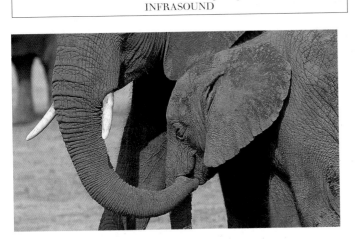

▲ SENSE OF TOUCH

A young elephant is touched by its mother or another close relative every few seconds. This constant reassurance keeps it from being frightened. Elephants also touch each other when they meet. They often stand resting with their bodies touching.

▲ QUICK LEARNERS

Some young working elephants learn to stop their bells ringing by pushing mud inside them. This allows the clever animals to steal food from farmers' fields without being heard.

Trunks

Imagine what it would be like if your nose and top lip were joined together and stretched into a long, bendy tube hanging down from your face. This is what an elephant's trunk must feel like. It can do everything your nose, lips, hand and arm can do – and more besides. An elephant uses its trunk to breathe, eat, drink, pick things up, throw things, feel, smell, fight and play, squirt water, mud and dust, greet and touch other elephants and make sounds. Not surprisingly, a baby elephant takes a long time to learn all the ways to use its trunk.

▲ DRINKING

An elephant cannot lower its head down to the ground to drink so it sucks up water with its trunk. Baby elephants drink with their mouths until they learn to use their trunks to squirt water into their mouths.

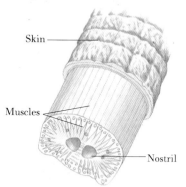

Skin

Muscles

Nostril

▲ A CLOSER LOOK

The two holes in the centre of the trunk are nostrils, through which the elephant breathes. Thousands of muscles pull against each other in different directions to move the trunk.

▲ TRUNK POWER

An African elephant coils its trunk around a branch to lift it off the ground. Elephants can lift whole tree trunks in this way. The powerful trunk has more than 100,000 muscles, which enable an elephant to lift large, heavy objects easily.

▲ TAKING A SHOWER

An elephant does not need to stand under a shower to be sprayed with water, mud or dust. Its trunk is like a built-in shower, able to cover almost its whole body as it reaches backwards over the head. Showering cools the elephant down and gets rid of insects.

▲ BENDY TRUNK

Elephants sometimes double up their trunks and rest them on their tusks. They can do this because the trunk has no bones inside it, just muscles, which makes it very flexible.

► TALL ORDER

African elephants use their long, stretchy trunks to pull leaves off the top branches of tall acacia trees. The highest leaves are the most juicy. The trunk is slightly telescopic, which means that, if necessary, it can be stretched out even longer than usual. The trunk can also be pushed into small holes or gaps between rocks to find hidden pools of water.

Asian elephant

African elephant

▲ TRUNK TIPS

The trunk of an African elephant has two fingers at the tip, while the Asian elephant has only one. These fingers can pick up an object as small as a leaf or a coin.

25

Keeping Cool

When we are hot, we lose heat through our skin, especially by sweating. An elephant cannot do this because it does not have sweat glands, so it must cool off in other ways. One way an elephant gets rid of excess body heat is by flapping its enormous ears. This increases the cooling flow of air over the body. The ears also work like a huge car radiator – they prevent overheating by letting heat escape from their vast surfaces. Elephants stay cool by spraying themselves with water, mud or dust. They also love bathing in water and rolling around in mud. The mud dries on the elephant's skin, providing a barrier against the sun's heat.

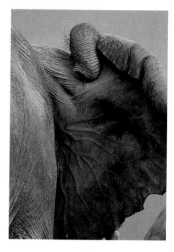

▲ RADIATOR EARS
The African bush elephant has the largest ears of all. It spends more time in open sunlight than the other species, and its large ears increase the amount of skin area through which heat can leave the body.

◀ SHADY TREES
On the African savanna, acacia trees have wide, flat tops. This makes them ideal sunshades for hot animals. Groups of elephants tend to seek out shade in the middle of the day when the sun is at its hottest.

▼ COOLING MUD

Elephants love to plaster themselves in mud, which changes their ordinary colours to vibrant reds, blacks, browns or yellows. Mud cools the skin, heals cuts, protects against insect bites and helps to stop the skin from getting dry and cracked.

▲ DUST SHOWER

Dust showers are popular with elephants. An earthy coating works like mud to protect the skin from the sun's heat. It also keeps skin in good condition.

▲ BATHTIME

Zoo elephants are often given a helping hand at bathtime. In a zoo, elephants may not have enough space to spray themselves with water or dust so the keepers regularly bathe them and brush their skin to keep it in good condition.

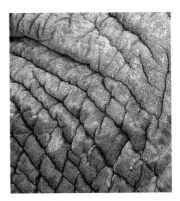

▲ COOL WRINKLES

An elephant's wrinkled skin helps it to keep cool. The wrinkles increase the overall surface area of the skin, so more heat can escape. They also trap cooling moisture.

27

Focus on

Elephants love water. They drink lots of it and enjoy jumping into lakes and rivers to play and splash around. Elephants are good swimmers and can easily cross rivers or swim out to sea to reach islands with fresh food. They drink at least once a day, or more often when water is available. When water is hard to find in the wild, elephants can be very sneaky, drinking from taps, pipes or water tanks. This usually causes damaged or broken pipes. However, elephants can go without water for up to two weeks.

SPLASHING ABOUT

Elephants spray each other with water, wrestle with their trunks and flop sideways with great splashes. Sometimes they turn upside down and poke the soles of their feet out of the water. All this play strengthens the bonds between individuals and keeps groups together.

TRUNK STRAW

These two elephants are refreshing themselves at a waterhole. Elephants drink by sucking in water through their trunk. They seal off the end with the finger or fingers at the end of the trunk. Then they lift the trunk to the mouth and squirt in the water.

CHAMPION SWIMMERS

Elephants are good at swimming even though they are so big. When an elephant swims underwater, it pokes its trunk above the water and breathes through it like a snorkel.

Water Babies

KEEPING CLEAN

Frequent bathing washes the build-up of mud and dust out of the cracks in an elephant's thick skin. Disease-carrying insects and parasites that feed off the elephant's skin are also washed off in the water.

WATER BABIES

In the water, baby elephants often hold on to the tail of the elephant in front for safety. They can easily be swept away by fast-flowing rivers. Baby elephants are also vulnerable to attack from crocodiles.

THIRST QUENCHER

An elephant needs to drink 70–90 litres of water a day. A full trunk of water holds about 5–10 litres. Incredibly, a very thirsty adult elephant can drink about 100 litres of water in 5 minutes.

On the Move

An elephant looks like a noisy, clumsy animal. In fact, it moves about quietly and is surprisingly agile. Forest elephants can quickly disappear into the trees like silent, grey ghosts. The secret of the elephant's silent movement is the way its foot is made. A fatty pad inside the foot cushions the impact of the foot on the ground. The sole then spreads out to take the weight of each step. Elephants usually walk slowly, at a rate of about 6kmph. They can run at more than 40kmph when angry or frightened, but only for a short distance. Elephants swim well too, and they often reach islands in lakes or off the coast. They are also good climbers, with a ridged sole that grips rough or steep ground well. However, elephants cannot jump. They would crush their legs on impact.

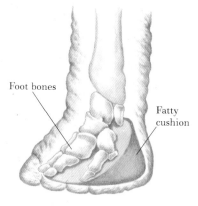

Foot bones

Fatty cushion

▲ FATTY FOOT

An elephant's enormous weight rests on the tips of its toes and on a fatty cushion that works like a giant shock absorber. This fatty shock absorber spreads out as the elephant puts its foot down and contracts as it lifts up its foot. On firm ground, the elephant leaves hardly any track marks.

Did you know? An elephant's foot measures up to 1.5m around.

◀ ELEPHANT WALK

An elephant walks and runs with shuffling steps. It cannot trot, canter or gallop. Occasionally, elephants walk backwards. They sometimes find this easier than turning around, which can be a difficult manoeuvre for an elephant.

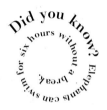

GRIPPING SOLES

The skin on the sole of an elephant's foot is thick and covered in cracks and deep ridges. These help it to grip rough ground effectively, rather like the treads on tyres or hiking boots.

Did you know? *Elephants can swim for six hours without a break.*

Royal Hunts
An Indian mythical story tells of King Khusraw, who was killed by his son Shirvieh. In the scene shown here, Shirvieh travels by elephant to the Royal Palace. Here he becomes caught up in a royal hunt. In India, people often rode elephants to hunt.

FOOTCARE

An elephant has a thorn removed from its foot. Elephants in captivity move about less than they do in the wild. As a result, their feet are less tough and need to be looked after. Toenails are not worn away either, so they have to be trimmed.

ON THE MARCH

A line of elephants crosses the savanna in Kenya. Elephants often march along in a row, sometimes with each elephant holding the tail of the one in front. Elephants usually walk about 25km a day, but in the hot deserts of Namibia in southwest Africa journeys of up to 195km a day have been recorded.

Indian Ocean

Somawathiya
National Park

Minneriya Giritale
Nature Reserve

Trikonamadu
Nature Reserve

Floodplain
National Park

Mahaweli
Ganga River

Wasgamuwa
National Park

main road

main road

protected areas ▢ planned extension
to protected areas

▲ ANIMAL CORRIDORS

Much of the land in Sri Lanka
is used for agriculture, so some
elephants live in protected
areas. They move between the
regions along special corridors
of land, in the same way that
people travel between cities
along motorways.

Elephant Migrations

Elephants do not have permanent homes. Every
year they make long journeys called migrations
to search for food and water. In the dry seasons,
elephants gather in large groups for feeding
migrations. They follow the same paths when
moving from one place to another year after year.
These paths are learnt by one generation of
elephants after another. Today, elephants have
been squeezed into smaller areas as human
beings take up more and more land. As a result,
elephant migrations are much shorter than they
used to be, although they may still cover
hundreds of kilometres.

ELEPHANT RAIDERS ▶

Farmers on the island of
Sumatra try to chase a
herd of elephants away
from their maize fields.
Migrating elephants
can do a lot of
damage to crops.

◀ ELEPHANT WELLS

During times of drought, elephants may dig
holes in dry stream beds. They use their
trunks, tusks and feet to reach water hidden
under the ground. Elephants need to drink
70-90 litres of water each day and have
been known to travel long distances of
up to 30km to reach a tiny patch of
rainfall. Elephant wells can be life-savers
for other wildlife that come to drink the
water after the elephants have gone.

LONG JOURNEYS ▶

African elephants on the savanna grasslands may wander over an area of more than 3,000 square km. The extent of their migrations depends on the weather and other conditions. Asian elephants living in forests migrate over smaller areas of about 100-300 square km.

◀ WATCHING FROM ABOVE

Migrating elephants can be followed by aeroplane in open country. Little or no rain falls during the dry season and the elephants tend to group together in places where water is available. The thirsty animals usually stay around a river valley or a swamp that still has water in it. In rainy seasons, elephants spread out over a wider area.

◀ ELEPHANT BARRIERS

Elephants will try anything to find a way through farmers' fences. They can use their tusks to break electric fence wires and even drop large rocks or logs on top of fences.

KEEPING TRACK ▶

Scientists in Africa fit a radio-collar to an elephant. This device tracks the animal's movements without disturbing its natural behaviour.

Feeding

Elephants are herbivores (plant-eaters). They eat more than 100 different kinds of plants and enjoy almost every part — from the leaves, twigs, bark and roots to the flowers, fruit, seeds and thorns. Plants do not contain much nutrition, however, so an elephant has to eat huge quantities to survive. It spends about 16 hours a day choosing, picking and eating its food. Millions of microscopic organisms live inside an elephant's gut, which help it to digest food. Even with the help of these organisms, half the food eaten by an elephant leaves the body undigested.

▲ **STRIPPING BARK**
An elephant munches on tree bark, which provides it with essential minerals and fibre. The elephant pushes its tusks under the bark to pull it away from the tree trunk. Then it peels off a strip of bark by pulling with its trunk.

◀ **EATING THORNS**
Elephants do not mind swallowing a mouthful of thorns — as long as some tasty leaves are attached to it! Leaves and thorns make up an important part of an elephant's diet as they stay green in the dry season long after the grasses have dried up. This is because trees and bushes have long roots to reach water deep underground.

▼ **GRASSY DIET**
Marshes are packed full of juicy grasses. About 30-60 per cent of an elephant's diet is grass. On dry land, an elephant may even beat grass against its leg to remove the soil before feeding.

Did you know? Elephants can become drunk by eating overripe fruit.

▶ **BABY FOOD**

Baby elephants often feed on the dung of adult elephants. They do this to pick up microscopic organisms to live inside their gut and help them digest food. Baby elephants learn what is good to eat by watching their mother and other relatives. They are also curious and like to try new types of food.

◀ **DUNG FOOD**

Elephant dung provides a feast for dung beetles and thousands of other insects. They lay their eggs in the dung, and the young feed on it when they hatch. Certain seeds only sprout in dung after having first passed through an elephant.

FOOD IN CAPTIVITY ▶

People make meals for captive elephants from grasses and molasses (a type of sugar). Zoo elephants eat food such as hay, bread, nuts, fruit, leaves, bark and vegetables. They need a huge pile of food every day – in the wild they eat 100-200kg of plants every day.

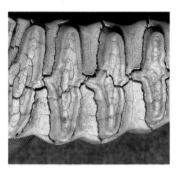

▲ **EARLY TOOTH**
This fossilized mammoth's tooth is 20cm long. The pattern of ridges on the tooth resembles that of an Asian elephant rather than an African elephant.

▲ **AFRICAN TOOTH**
The ridges on an African elephant's tooth are lozenge (diamond) shaped. The scientific name of this elephant, *Loxodonta*, means lozenge teeth.

▲ **ASIAN ELEPHANT TOOTH**
The ridges on the surface of an elephant's tooth act like scissor blades. They cut up food as the elephant chews.

Teeth

An elephant's front teeth are its tusks. They stick out from the mouth. An elephant also has molar teeth inside its mouth. The tusks are only in the top jaw, but the molars are in both the top and the bottom jaw. Two molars sit on each side of the mouth, each one weighing more than a brick. Sharp ridges along the top of the molars grind up tough plants. Tusks grow continuously, but molars gradually wear down and drop out. New teeth develop behind the old ones and slowly move forward along the jaw to take their place. An elephant gets through six sets of molar teeth in a lifetime – that is 24 molar teeth altogether. Each new tooth is bigger than the one before. After the sixth replacement set, the elephant is no longer able to chew its food properly.

▲ **CHEWING UP FOOD**
An elephant uses just four huge teeth inside its mouth at any one time. It has two in the top jaw and two in the bottom jaw. Its lower jaws move back and forth to chew. This pulls and pushes the food against the grinding ridges of the molar teeth.

▶ CONVEYOR-BELT TEETH

An elephant's teeth come through at the back of the mouth, move forward and wear out at the front. Once a set of molars has lost its effectiveness, replacement sets of molars are in reserve, ready to push in from behind. The first teeth are replaced at 1-2 years old, the second at 3-4 years, the third at 8-10 years, the fourth around 20-25 years and the fifth at 35-40. The sixth set of molars must last the elephant for the rest of its life.

Old molar about to drop out.

New molar.

Jaw bone.

Parts of the front molar break off.

Molars develop at the back of the jaw.

◀ OPEN WIDE

The positions of the molar teeth inside the mouth of an African elephant can be seen by peering down its throat. The mouth is relatively small and delicate and the tongue is fleshy.

Did you know? An adult elephant's tooth can be 30cm long and weigh 4kg.

▲ LONG IN THE TOOTH

Scientists work out the age of an elephant by looking at its teeth. When the animal loses its last tooth, it cannot chew its food properly and soon dies of malnutrition.

Focus on

An elephant's day follows a regular pattern of feeding, sleeping and travelling to new feeding areas. Meeting, greeting and communicating with other elephants is an important part of every day and interrupts other activities from time to time. Feeding takes up most of the time – about 16 hours a day. They also need to drink a lot of water and bathe to cool off. Elephants sleep twice a day, once for a few hours at noon and again in the early hours of the morning. They usually sleep standing up, but sometimes they lie on their sides.

LIQUID REFRESHMENT

Elephants usually drink only once or twice a day. As they stroll along in their endless search for food, they have to make sure they do not wander too far from the nearest waterhole. Sometimes their migration routes follow rivers.

MEAL TIME

When an elephant feeds, it may close its eyes or gaze off into the distance. Seeing its food is less important to the animal than touching and smelling it. The elephant uses its trunk to feel for food.

STICKING TOGETHER

Adult elephants help babies to cross rivers. Young elephants have to keep up with the rest of the herd as it wanders over large areas searching for food and water. However, adult elephants cooperate with each other to protect and guide the young of the herd. When danger is sensed, the group forms a tight circle around the calves. The matriarch (female leader) faces the direction of the threat.

Daily Life

AT PLAY

Elephant calves play together for part of every day. They chase, push and climb over other babies and wrestle with their trunks. These playful calves are testing out their strength and learning to live in the group.

TIME FOR A NAP

Usually, elephants sleep standing up, supported by their firm, rigid legs. They may rest their trunks on the ground while they snooze. At other times, elephants sleep lying on their sides. When they do this, they have been known to make pillows of grass for themselves. Sleeping elephants have also been heard snoring.

NIGHT REFRESHMENT

A group of elephants has a cool night-time drink at a water hole in Namibia, southwest Africa. Elephants use their keen senses of smell, touch and hearing to find their way in the dark. When feeding at night, they also make rumbling noises to let each other know where they are. Family members like to eat at the same time.

Living Together

An elephant family group is made up of related females and their offspring. Each family is led by an older, dominant female known as the matriarch. She makes all the decisions for the group. Her experience, learned over many years, is very important in keeping the family healthy and safe. Female elephants never leave the matriarchal unit unless it becomes too big. Then smaller groups break away and are led by the eldest daughters. Bulls (male elephants) leave their family group when they are between 10 and 16 years old. When they are adults, only the strongest males mate with the females. Bulls spend most of their lives in small, all-male groups (comprising two or three animals) or wander on their own. Each family group has close links with up to five other families in the same area. These linked family units, together with groups of adult bulls, make up a herd.

▲ LITTLE LEARNERS
Young elephant calves copy the adults of the family to learn where to find water and food. If they are in trouble, a big sister, a cousin or an aunt is always around to help.

▼ THE MATRIARCH
Usually, the oldest and largest adult female becomes the matriarch (female leader). The rest of the group rely on her. She controls when they eat, drink and rest. She also protects them from dangers and controls family members who misbehave.

Sire bull
(male parent)

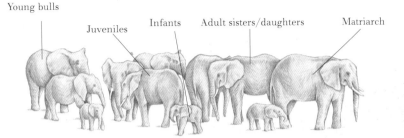

Young bulls

Juveniles   Infants   Adult sisters/daughters   Matriarch

▲ AFRICAN FAMILY

A family of African elephants usually consists of a matriarch, her adult daughters and sisters, their calves and a number of young males and females. Bulls may sometimes join the family for mating but they do not stay with it for long. They soon leave to resume their solitary lives.

◄ ASIAN FAMILIES

Elephants in Asia live in smaller groups than African elephants. Asian families have between four and eight members, although as many as 10-20 individuals may stay in touch.

◄ ALONE

Young bulls have a lot to learn once they leave the safety of their families. Often, they follow older males (patriarchs) around, and sometimes they have mock fights. However, males do not form such strong social bonds with each other as the females in family groups do. As a result, some bulls lead entirely solitary lives.

41

Communication

Everyone knows the loud trumpeting sound that elephants make. They trumpet when they are excited, surprised, angry or lost. This sound is just one way in which elephants can communicate with one another. They also touch, smell, give off chemical signals and perform visual displays, such as the position of the ears and the trunk. Their sense of smell can even tell them about another elephant's health. Elephants also make a wide range of low, rumbling sounds that carry for many kilometres through forests and grasslands. Different rumbles might mean "Where are you?" or "Let's go" or "I want to play". Females can signal when they are ready to mate, and family members can warn each other of danger.

▲ **ELEPHANT GREETING**
When elephants meet, they touch each other with their trunks, smell each other and rumble greeting sounds. Frightened elephants also touch others for reassurance.

▶ **BODY LANGUAGE**
Elephants send visual signals by moving their ears and trunk. Spreading the ears wide makes the elephant look bigger. This sends a message to a potential attacker to stay away. The elephant also stands up extra tall to increase the threat. It raises its tusks and shakes its head, making its ears crack like whips against its sides.

Did you know?
Humans can only hear about one third of the sounds an elephant makes.

42

◀ SPECIAL SOUNDS

An elephant makes its familiar high-pitched trumpeting call. Elephants also make a variety of crying, bellowing, screaming, snorting and rumbling sounds. Asian elephants make sounds that African elephants do not, and many of their rumbles last for longer. There are over 20 different kinds of rumble, with females making many more rumbling sounds than males. Females sometimes make rumbling calls when they are together, but male elephants do not do this.

▲ ALARM SIGNALS

This nervous baby elephant is interested in the crocodiles lying on the river bank. It raises its ears, either in alarm or as a threat to the crocodiles. If a baby calls out in distress, its relatives rush to its side, with rumbles of reassurance and comforting touches with their trunks.

▲ TOUCH AND SMELL

An elephant's skin is very sensitive, and touch is an important way of communicating feelings in elephant society. Smells also pass on useful messages, such as when a female or male is ready to mate.

Babar
One of the most famous elephants in children's literature is Babar the elephant king. He was created by French writer Jean de Brunhoff. Babar rules over the Land of the Elephants with the help of his wife Queen Celeste and his old friend General Cornelius. He fights wars with the rhinos, escapes from the circus and has many other exciting adventures.

43

JUST PRACTISING

Young bulls sometimes have pretend fights. They push and charge at each other, clash their tusks and wrestle with their heads.

Male and female elephants live separately most of the time. When young male elephants become adults (at between 10 and 16 years), they are chased away from their family herd. Young bulls then form loose bonds with other males and only visit family groups occasionally. They learn from older males how to fight other males, search for females and mate with them. Bulls compete with each other to become the dominant (top) male elephant in their area. Only dominant bulls mate with the females. This helps to produce healthy, strong babies. Bulls stay near a family herd only when a female is ready to mate, but they will also help to defend the herd.

IN MUSTH

About once every year, adult bulls go through a period of unpredictable, aggressive behaviour called musth. A bull in musth oozes a sticky fluid from the side of his face.

FINDING A MATE

Female elephants prefer to mate with the biggest bulls. Males keep growing until they are aged between 35 and 45 years. Females stop growing at about 25 years.

Bull Elephants

ESTABLISHING CONTROL

Adult bull elephants have mock-fights with each other to decide who is dominant and most likely to mate with the females. The bulls push and wrestle with their heads, trunks and tusks, sometimes even lifting their opponent's front legs off the ground. Eventually, the weaker bull gives up and is chased away. .

BACHELOR HERDS

Young bulls sometimes form small groups for a while, called bachelor herds. These groupings are only temporary, however, and bulls lead a lonely life compared with females.

FIGHTING BULLS

In ancient India, people liked to watch bull elephants fighting. They used bulls in musth because the bulls were then in a fighting mood.

Courtship

Male and female animals meet each other and select a mate by a process called courtship. For adult bulls this can happen at any time, but a cow can only mate on a few days every 16 weeks. During this time, she gives off special scents and makes sounds to attract bulls. When the bulls get close, she may begin walking with her head held high while looking back over her shoulder. A bull then follows her around, stroking her with his trunk. At the same time, he tries to chase away other bulls. Large bulls in musth (a period of heightened sexual desire) are best at doing this as they put all their energy into mating. Eventually, the cow may allow the bull to mate with her. The pair stay together for a few hours or a few days.

MEETING UP

An African bull elephant meets up with the cows in a group when they are ready to mate. A cow is first ready to mate from about 8-18 years of age, depending on the environment she lives in and the amount of food available.

THE THRILL OF THE CHASE

During African elephant courtship, bulls may chase after cows. Depending on her mood, the cow may stop and allow the bull to mate with her, or just keep running. Cows can run faster than the large, heavy bulls.

▲ TESTING THE WATER

When a female is on heat (ready to mate), her urine has a different smell. This musth bull is smelling the female's urine to find out if it has the mating smell. He will curl the tip of his trunk into his mouth to blow the scent over two small openings in the roof of the mouth. These openings detect the scent of a female on heat.

▲ COURTSHIP CONTACT

Elephants often touch each other with their trunks during courtship. African bulls may lay their trunk and tusks along the female's back. In Asia, a bull and a cow elephant face each other and twine their trunks together.

▲ MATING

During the act of mating, the bull elephant stands on his back legs and supports his huge weight on the cow's back. Mating can last for anything up to three minutes and may take place every two or three hours for a few days.

Birth and Babies

Female elephants are pregnant for nearly two years. They give birth to their first calf when they are between 10 and 20 years old. After that, they can produce a calf every 4-6 years until the age of about 50, when the birth rate slows down. A female elephant can have between 5 and 12 babies in a lifetime. Female elephants in the same group often have babies at about the same time and look after their young together. In areas where dry seasons make food hard to find, most births take place during rainy seasons. A young calf is highly vulnerable. Its mother feeds it milk for up to six years and protects it from enemies such as lions and tigers, yet about a third of all calves do not survive. Some drown or are crushed by falling trees.

▲ **BIRTH TIME**
When a baby elephant is born, it emerges from the cow in a protective covering called a birth sac. The other females sniff the newcomer and softly touch it all over, while rumbling with excitement.

A baby elephant practises using its trunk.

▲ **TRUNK TRICKS**
Baby elephants are curious and inquisitive. They want to touch and feel everything with their trunk. At first, they cannot control their long, wobbly nose. They trip over it or suck on it – just as human babies suck their thumbs. It takes months of practice to learn how to use the trunk.

▶ **MILK BAR**
A calf suckles milk from its mother's breasts with its mouth. The milk is thin and watery, but very nourishing. Babies put on weight at a rate of 10-20 kg per month.

◀ LEARNING FAST

A young elephant has to master giving itself a dust bath. It must also learn to pick up and carry things with its trunk, drink, feed and have a mudbath. If a young elephant cannot reach water, the mother sucks up water in her trunk and squirts it down her baby's throat.

Did you know? A newborn baby elephant weighs more than an average-sized adult human.

GUIDING TRUNK ▶

At first, a baby elephant sticks close to its mother night and day. It is always within reach of a comforting touch from her strong, guiding trunk. The mother encourages her baby, helps it to keep up with other members of the herd and often pulls it back if it starts to stray. Baby elephants will die quickly if they are left on their own.

▲ PROPER FOOD

After a few months, calves begin to eat plants. At first, a calf may put its trunk into its mother's mouth to test out which plants are edible.

▲ HELPFUL RELATIVES

The survival of both mothers and calves depends greatly on the support of the family group. Each member takes part in bringing up the babies so that young elephants learn to care for calves, too. This support also gives the mother a break.

Focus on

Giving birth can be quite a dangerous time for elephants because the pregnant female is particularly vulnerable to attack. To protect her, other females may form a large circle around her. More experienced relatives, known as midwives, usually help with the birth. The whole birth process takes only about an hour. Within two hours of birth, the calf usually begins to take its first shaky steps. The mother often takes it to meet the rest of the family group. The other elephants greet the arrival of the new calf with great excitement.

1 Most female elephants squat down to give birth. Occasionally, they give birth lying down. Cows are often restless during the time it takes for the calf to emerge. The other females may trumpet and scream to keep away predators.

2 The female elephant has to push as hard as possible to force the calf out of her body. Finally, the calf begins to emerge from between its mother's back legs. A female relative usually stands nearby to act as a midwife and help the struggling mother at this difficult time.

Giving Birth

3 Sometimes a baby elephant is born feet first. It emerges still partly inside the protective sac in which it has spent the last 22 months within its mother's belly. Amazingly, the delivery of the calf is fairly quick and lasts only about half a minute. After the birth, the midwife encourages the mother to push out the afterbirth (the material that helps support, feed and protect the baby whilst it is in the womb).

4 The mother and the midwife together remove the sticky birth sac from around the newborn baby. The mother then eats the afterbirth, which is full of vitamins and nutritious hormones. They help her to produce milk as quickly as possible in order to feed her newborn calf. She usually recovers her strength after a short time.

5 A calf can usually stand on its feet within about an hour of its birth. Nevertheless, its mother helps support it with her feet and trunk for a while longer. Once the newborn calf gets to its feet, it is guided to its mother's nipple for its first drink of milk. Her nipples are situated on her belly, between her front legs.

Growing Up

A baby elephant is brought up by its family in a fun-loving, easy-going and caring environment – in spite of the dangers. At first, a calf spends a lot of time with its mother. Then, as it grows older and stronger, it is allowed more freedom to explore and it begins to make friends with other calves. Calves spend a lot of time playing together. They can do this because they feed on their mother's milk and do not have to find food all day. Gradually the calf learns all the skills it needs to survive on its own.

▲ **BROTHERS AND SISTERS**
An older calf may cling to its mother for reassurance even after it has learnt to feed itself. A female elephant may have calves every four to six years. Usually, just when the first calf can feed itself, another one arrives.

Did you know? Female elephants become adult in nine or ten years but males mature a few years later.

◀ **MOTHER'S MILK**
A calf drinks its mother's milk until it is between four and six years old. By then, the mother usually needs her milk for the next baby. Even so, calves as old as eight have been known to push a younger brother or sister out of the way to steal a drink.

◀ PLAYTIME

A growing elephant learns a lot simply by playing. Male elephants push and shove each other to test their strength. Females play games with lots of chasing, such as tag. Both males and females like to mess about in mud, dust or water.

▲ PROTECTING THE YOUNG

All the adults in a family are protective of the young. They shade calves from the sun and stand guard over them while they sleep. Small calves are vulnerable to attack from many predators, including poisonous snakes.

Ganesh

In the Hindu religion of India, Ganesh is the elephant-headed god of wisdom and the remover of obstacles. Ganesh's father, the god Siva, is said to have cut off Ganesh's head. His mother, the goddess Parvati, was so angry that she forced Siva to give her son a new head. This new head turned out to be that of an elephant. Hindus seek good luck from Ganesh before the start of important business.

◀ LOTS OF MOTHERS

Aunties, also called allomothers, take a special interest in the upbringing of calves. They wake the calf up when it is time to travel, help it if it gets stuck in mud and protect it from danger.

Life and Death

Whilst elephant calves often fall prey to crocodiles and big cats, it is hard to imagine how an animal as big and powerful as an adult elephant can be harmed. Adult elephants have no serious predators apart from people, who kill them for their ivory tusks or destroy their habitats. Yet elephants can also be killed by diseases, accidents, droughts or floods, just like any other animal. When an elephant dies, members of its family try to pick it up. They may throw dust or leaves on the body and stand over it for hours. Elephants also seem to remember where family members have died.

▲ DROUGHT

Elephants gather by rivers and swamps during a drought. Food and water is in short supply at this time. For heavy water users like elephants, lack of water can be fatal. Drought is the most likely cause of death in African elephants after being hunted by humans.

Did you know?
Elephants can recognise the body of a dead relative.

◄ OLD AGE

Older elephants move less quickly than others. The group slows down to wait for them. When an elephant has worn down its sixth and final set of teeth, feeding becomes difficult. It cannot grind up and digest its food properly. Whenever possible, it feeds on soft, watery vegetation at swamps and lakes. Eventually, feeding becomes impossible altogether, and the elephant collapses and dies from malnutrition.

▶ FASCINATING BONES

Elephants appear to be fascinated by the bones of dead elephants. They feel, sniff and scatter them about. Sometimes, the animals pull out the tusks from the skull and smash them. They may even carry bones about in their mouths for a time or bury them. Chewing bones may also be a way of obtaining the mineral calcium, which is contained in bones and teeth.

An elephant gently touches the body of a dying family member to try to rouse it.

◀ RESPECTING THE DEAD

A dying elephant is comforted by another family member, who touches it gently with its trunk. If a family member dies, the group often lingers for days, apparently showing respect for the dead. They comfort any bereaved calves. If a young calf dies, the mother may carry it about on her tusks for a while. When elephants come across the body of a dead elephant, they smell or touch it all over.

▲ KILLING AND CULLING

In the past, people used to kill elephants for sport. Today, this is usually banned or strictly controlled, although poachers still shoot elephants illegally. Elephants may also be killed when there are too many of them in an area and there is nowhere else for them to go. This is called culling. The idea is to leave space for a smaller number of elephants to survive.

▲ ELEPHANT GRAVEYARDS

In stories and films such as *Tarzan of the Apes*, elephants slip away to secret communal places to die. The belief in elephant graveyards arose when people found large collections of bones in one place. Actually, these places were probably the last watering holes of drought-stricken elephants.

55

Ancestors

The two species of elephant today are the surviving members of a once-huge group of animals. The early members looked nothing like elephants, however. *Moeritherium*, which lived 50-60 million years ago, was a dog-sized animal with no trunk. This creature evolved into a larger animal called *Palaeomastodon*, with tusks, long lips and jaws for feeding. The first true elephant ancestor, *Stegodon*, evolved about 12 million years ago. It gave rise to the African and Asian elephant, as well as the now-extinct mammoth.

EARLIEST ANCESTOR

Moeritherium was a small animal that lived in and around lakes and swamps about 50-60 million years ago. It had nostrils instead of a trunk, which were high on its face for breathing whilst submerged. Its eyes were also set quite high, similar to those of a hippo, to allow it to see easily whilst in the water. *Moeritherium* had sturdy legs, like an elephant, and small tusks.

GOMPHOTHERIUM ▶

This distant elephant ancestor was up to 3m tall. Its skull was longer than that of a modern elephant, and it had tusks in both the top and bottom jaws. The lower jaw was longer so that the short lower tusks reached out as far as the upper ones.

◀ *STEGODON GANESA*

Stegodon ganesa lived in India and is named after the Hindu elephant-headed god Ganesh. It probably lived in forests and ate bamboo shoots and leaves. The long tusks of this animal were parallel along most of their length and grew very close together. The family to which this elephant belonged was similar to, but distinct from, true elephants. It died out about one million years ago.

▲ MASTODONS

Creatures known as
mastodons were
more common
than mammoths
in the woodlands of
North America. They lived more than 10,000 years ago and
were about the same size as an Asian elephant, with long black
-brown hair. Some mastodons had two small tusks in the lower
jaw as well as the big, curved tusks in the top jaw.

The Cyclops
In Greek legend, Cyclops
were fierce giants with only
one eye. The legend may
have been based on the
fossilized skull of a
mastodon found in Greece.
The huge nose opening
could have been mistaken for
a large, central eye socket.

▶ WOOLLY MAMMOTHS

These elephant relatives lived
in cold areas. They had long,
woolly coats to protect them
from freezing temperatures.
Mammoths
lived at the
same time as
early humans and died
out about 10,000 years ago.

▼ PRESERVED SKULL

Mammoth skeletons, including skulls, have
been found in Asia. From their preserved
flesh, we can work out that mammoths had
small ears. They would have
helped to stop the
animal from losing
valuable body
heat in very
cold areas.

▲ CAVE PAINTING

Stone-age people painted pictures of mammoths
on cave walls, many of which can still be seen
today. These early humans may have dug pits to
trap mammoths or driven them over cliffs.

Relatives and Namesakes

Elephants do not look like any other mammals alive today, yet they have some unlikely-looking relatives. In fact their closest living relatives are manatees and dugongs, which live in rivers, swamps and seas. Another animal that is closely related to elephants is about the size of a squirrel. It is called a hyrax and lives among rocks or in trees. The tiny elephant shrews of Africa may also be distant relatives. Evidence for these relationships comes from studying fossils and from comparing the bones and internal organs of living animals. Scientists also compare the DNA of different animals. DNA is a chemical that is passed on from parent to offspring. It is very similar in closely related animal groups.

▲ ELEPHANT SHREWS
This tiny mammal is named after its trunk-like snout, which it uses to find insects to eat. The DNA of elephant shrews is similar to the DNA of elephants, which suggests that they are related.

▼ HYRAXES
The hyrax has several features in common with the elephant. For example, both have ridges on their teeth and similar foot bones.

◄ DUGONGS
These elephant relations live in the western Pacific and the Indian oceans. They are the only vegetarian sea mammals. Dugongs, like elephants, are social animals and live in groups. Male dugongs also have tusk-like front teeth.

Mermaids

In seafaring legend, mermaids and mermen were strange creatures with human bodies and fish tails. They caused shipwrecks, floods and other disasters. These legends may have begun when sailors first saw manatees or dugongs. These animals suckle their young in a similar way to humans, yet the fish-like tail of a manatee or a dugong looks like that of a mermaid or merman.

▲ MANATEES

The manatee, like its relative the dugong, is a plump, slow-moving, vegetarian. Manatees and dugongs are sometimes called sea cows. This is because they graze on sea plants just as cows graze on land plants. Sea cows swim as whales do, using their flippers and tail.

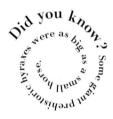

Did you know? Some giant prehistoric hyraxes were as big as a small horse.

▶ ELEPHANT SEAL

Despite its name, the elephant seal is not related to the elephant. It gets its name from the long, trunk-like nose of the male. Female elephant seals do not have the huge, swollen noses. During the breeding season, male elephant seals roar at their rivals and the nose works like a loudspeaker.

Life with People

For thousands of years, people have hunted elephants for their meat or ivory. They have also captured and trained elephants to carry out tasks such as fighting in battles, carrying loads and pulling heavy logs out of forests. Elephants are also used in cultural and religious ceremonies, while others are trained to entertain people in circuses or zoos. Many parts of dead elephants are used in traditional Chinese medicines, including eyeballs to treat eye diseases. Today, both scientists and tourists ride on the backs of elephants in order to study or watch other animals in the wild.

▲ ZOO ELEPHANTS
Zoos and wildlife parks can help elephant conservation through education, research, fund raising and careful breeding. The best zoos keep small herds in large grassy paddocks to imitate the elephants' own habitats.

◀ ON SAFARI
In Africa, some elephants are used to take tourists on wildlife trips called safaris. The elephants can easily walk through tall grass and over rough ground where vehicles cannot go. Also, dangerous animals such as tigers and rhinos respect the elephant's great size and strength.

◄ CEREMONIAL ELEPHANTS

These elephants are taking part in an elephant march in South India. This is a competition to decide which of the elephant riders have the most colourful and striking umbrellas. Another Indian festival features a parade of colourfully painted elephants draped with rich cloth.

▲ TOURIST ELEPHANTS

In the past, hunters with guns shot animals from the backs of elephants. Now the shooting is done with cameras by tourists on organized elephant safaris. In Africa, fewer elephants are used for this purpose than in Asia. This is because there is no tradition in Africa of training elephants for work and ceremonial purposes.

◄ ELEPHANTS IN WAR

Ancient Indian war elephants wore armour and were used to trample on the enemy. Soldiers rode on top of the elephants in a wooden castle known as a howdah.

▲ CIRCUS ELEPHANTS

Elephants have appeared in circuses since Roman times. They can be trained to perform tricks, although circuses with animals are becoming increasingly rare today.

Focus on a

Elephants were first tamed and made to work about 5,000 years ago. In Asia today between 14,000 and 17,000 elephants (about a third of all elephants in Asia) are put into service. In the past, they were caught in the wild and tamed before being trained. Now, most working elephants are born in captivity. Training usually begins when the elephant is about ten years old. It finishes when the animal is about 25. The process can be cruel. The elephant may be tied to a tree without food or water for days in order to break its spirit.

SADDLE UP
This elephant is being trained in Thailand, southeast Asia. It has to learn to accept a rider on its back and must wear a wooden saddle with chains for dragging logs. Trained elephants may be used to help train others.

BATHTIME
Working elephants enjoy a daily bath. It helps the keeper and the elephant build up a friendship and learn to trust each other.

ELEPHANT-BACK
Elephants are still the best form of transport in many areas. They move through hilly forests and cross rivers more easily than trucks. Elephants do not burn costly fuel or pollute the air, and they have longer working lives than many machines.

Working Life

HEAVY LOAD

Some elephants today are used to carry loads in hilly areas where it is difficult for vehicles to move easily. An adult elephant can carry a load weighing up to 500kg on its back. Elephants are not well suited for heavy carrying, however. They have weak shoulders and high ridged backbones.

MAHOUTS

A working elephant usually has one trainer or handler for its whole working life. In India trainers are called mahouts. In Myanmar (Burma) they are called oozies. The trainers control their elephants with up to 60 words of command. In addition, they touch the elephant with their feet or hands. A spiked stick called an ankus is used during training to help reinforce commands.

LOGGING

In southeast Asia, elephants are used to transport heavy logs. Many people are concerned that the logging industry is destroying the forest homes of many animals including elephants themselves.

Facing Extinction

Today, elephants are in great danger. Wildlife experts warn that the species faces extinction and must be protected if it is to survive in the future. Asian elephants are most at risk, with only between 36,000 and 44,000 individuals left in the wild. In Asia, the main cause of the decline is humans taking the elephants' land. Activities such as building houses, mining, growing crops and constructing dams take up a lot of space. In Africa, the biggest threat is the ivory trade. African elephants have bigger tusks than Asian elephants and are therefore more sought after. Although the ivory trade was banned in 1989, it will take a long time for elephant numbers to recover.

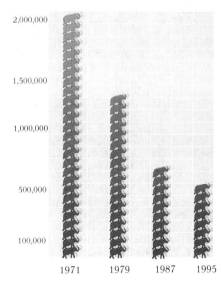

2,000,000
1,500,000
1,000,000
500,000
100,000

1971   1979   1987   1995

ON THE DECLINE
Between 1971 and 1989, the number of elephants in Africa more than halved, from 2 million to 609,000. Up to 300 were killed each day. Over 90% of these elephants were killed illegally by poachers.

Did you know? Elephant meat is sold as food in certain Asian countries.

IVORY BONFIRE
In 1989, the Kenyan government burned US $3.6 million worth of ivory on this huge bonfire. They did this in order to support the worldwide ban on the trade in ivory. However, poachers will go on killing elephants illegally as long as people are prepared to pay huge sums of money for the tusks.

◀ **WHITE GOLD**

People have carved ivory for tens of thousands of years. Carvings in mammoth ivory have been found that date back 27,000 years. In ancient Egypt, both hippo and elephant ivory was carved. Ivory makes an ideal material for trade because even a small amount has a very high value. It is easy to carve but also hard enough to last, with a smooth, cool surface.

▲ **POACHING**

When poachers kill elephants, they only want the tusks. They leave the rest of the elephant to rot. Before the ban on ivory trading, an African poacher could earn hundreds of dollars for just one pair of tusks. It would take the poacher a year to earn this much money in an ordinary job.

▲ **TOO MANY ELEPHANTS**

African elephant feet are sometimes sold to raise money for conservation. These animals were legally killed in a National Park where elephant numbers had grown too high.

▼ **ELEPHANTS OR PEOPLE?**

These elephants are invading a farmer's home and fields in Kenya, east Africa. The human population of Kenya is expected to double by the year 2020, putting enormous pressure on the land. Finding enough land for both people and elephants will be a problem. Elephants will not be able to roam freely, as they have been able to do in the past, but will be confined to special areas.

Conservation

Elephants need to be conserved if the species is to survive. Many African and Asian countries have set aside areas of land called national parks or nature reserves. Here, elephants are protected from the threat of poachers. This is not a perfect solution, however. Elephants in reserves are so well protected that their numbers steadily increase. Eventually, they eat themselves out of food. The rangers are then forced to kill some elephants to let others live. Other conservation efforts include keeping elephants on game ranches and banning trade in ivory. Alternatives to ivory, such as plastics, resins and the nuts of a South American palm tree, are less damaging to wildlife.

▲ **CAPTIVE BREEDING**
A zoo elephant has its foot cleaned with a hoof knife. Zoos play a role in conserving animals. However, elephants are not often bred in zoos because bulls are difficult to handle and can be dangerous.

▲ **WALRUS WORRIES**
When the trade in elephant ivory was banned in 1989, poachers turned their attention to walrus ivory instead. During 1989, poachers in speedboats shot at least 12,000 Alaskan walruses, whose tusks can grow almost a metre long.

▲ **POACHING PATROLS**
Guards in a national park in southern Africa hold wire traps left by poachers. Protecting elephants from poachers is dangerous work. As well as removing traps left for elephants, guards may become involved in gun battles as poachers try to kill elephants.

ELEPHANT TRAVELS

Sometimes, elephants are moved to areas where they have better chances of survival. Moving elephants is not an easy thing to do, however. Getting these enormous, heavy animals into a truck or an aeroplane can be a tricky business. Sometimes a whole family is moved, which helps these sensitive animals get over the trauma. They then settle into their new home more easily.

SUPPORT GROUPS

Conservation groups such as Elefriends in the UK raise money to help conservation work in the wild. They also persuade people not to buy and trade in ivory.

ORPHAN BABIES

With a great deal of patience, care and understanding, orphaned baby elephants can be raised in National Parks in Africa and returned to the wild. Raising a baby elephant is just as hard work as raising a baby human.

TOURIST TRAPS

Tourists pay to watch elephants in national parks. This money is used to help run the parks and look after the elephants. It is also used to improve the lives of people living nearby. Many of these people have given up their land to save the elephants.

Big Cats

Rhonda Klevansky

Consultant: Dr Nigel Dunstone,
Durham University

What is a Cat?

Cats are native to every continent except Australia and Antarctica. All cats are mammals with fine fur that is often beautifully marked. They are skilled hunters and killers with strong agile bodies, acute senses and sharp teeth and claws. Cats are stealthy and intelligent animals and many are solitary and very secretive. Although cats vary in size from the domestic (house) cat to the huge Siberian tiger, they all belong to the same family, the Felidae. This means that both wild and domestic cats look alike and behave in very similar ways. In all, there are 38 different species of cat.

▲ **LONG TAIL**
A cat's long tail helps it to balance as it runs. Cats also use their tails to signal their feelings to other cats.

All cats have short, rounded heads.

Whiskers help a cat to feel its surroundings.

The body of a cat is muscular and supple, with a broad, powerful chest.

▲ **BIG BITE**
As this tiger yawns it reveals its sharp teeth and strong jaws that can give a lethal bite. Cats use their long, curved canine teeth for killing prey.

▲ **BIG CATS**
Cats are very specialized flesh eaters. They are the perfect carnivore, with excellent hearing and eyesight. Their curved, razor-sharp claws, used for catching and holding prey, are retractable. This means they can be pulled into the paws to protect them when running. The hair covering a cat's paws and pads helps it to move silently.

70

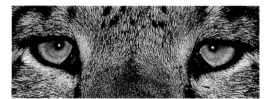

▲ NIGHT SIGHT

The pupils (dark centres) of cats' eyes close to a slit or small circle during the day to keep out the glare. At night they open up to let in as much light as possible. This enables a cat to see well at night as well as during the day.

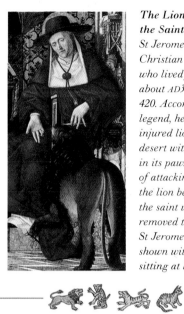

The Lion and the Saint
St Jerome was a Christian scholar who lived from about AD331 to 420. According to legend, he found an injured lion in the desert with a thorn in its paw. Instead of attacking him, the lion befriended the saint when he removed the thorn. St Jerome is often shown with a lion sitting at his feet.

Very soft fur is kept clean by regular grooming with the tongue and paws.

A long tail helps the cat to balance when it runs and leaps on prey.

Did you know? Some Arctic peoples believe that cats represent the spirits of the dead.

Cats walk on their toes, not on the whole foot.

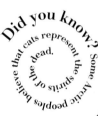

Large ears draw in sounds.

CATS EARS ▶

A cat's ears are set high on its head. This gives a keen hunter the best possible chance of picking up sounds. The ears have a rounded shape, which enables sounds to be picked up from many directions. Cats can also rotate their ears to face towards the source of a sound.

The Big Cats

Scientists classify (arrange) the members of the cat family into related groups. The two main groups are small cats (the domestic cat and many wild cats) and the big cats (the tiger, lion, leopard, snow leopard and jaguar). The clouded leopard and the cheetah are each grouped separately, but many people regard them as big cats. Big cats differ from small cats not only because of their size. Big cats can roar, but small cats cannot. Small cats purr. They have a special bone, the hyoid, at the base of their tongues that enables them to breath and purr at the same time. Big cats have elastic cartilage instead and can only purr when they breathe out. The puma is in fact a very large small cat. It is included here because of its size.

▲ **LION**
The lion is the only social cat and lives in a family group called a pride. Adult male lions, unlike other big cats, have a long, thick mane of hair. Female lions do not have manes.

▲ **PUMA**
The puma is also called the cougar or mountain lion. Although it is about the same size as a leopard, a puma is a small cat because it can purr. Pumas live in North and South America.

◀ **CHEETAH**
The tall cheetah is built like a slim athlete and is able to chase prey at great speed. Cheetahs are different from other cats in that they have retractable claws, but no sheaths to cover them. It was thought that cheetahs were related to dogs, but scientists now think that their closest cousins are pumas.

▲ LEOPARD

The leopard is built for bursts of speed and for climbing trees. Heavier than a cheetah, this cat is not as large and bulky as a tiger or a lion. Its spotted coat helps to hide the cat as it hunts in wooded grassland. Black leopards are called panthers. They are the same species, but their spots are hidden.

▲ SNOW LEOPARD

Snow leopards are a different species from true leopards. These rare cats have very thick coats to keep them warm in the high mountains of central Asia. They have very long tails, which help them to balance as they leap from rock to rock in their mountainous surroundings.

▼ JAGUAR

The jaguar is sometimes confused with a leopard, but it is stockier and not as agile. This big cat lives throughout South America in forested habitats where it needs power to climb rather than speed to run.

▲ TIGER

The most powerful and largest of all the big cats is the tiger. A tiger reaches on average a length of over 2m and weighs 230kg. The biggest tigers live in the snowy forests of Siberia in Russia. A few tigers also live in tropical forest reserves and swamps in Asia.

Did you know? Although lions are called the King of the Jungle they do not live there.

Bones and Teeth

The skeleton of a cat gives it its shape and has 230 bones (a human has 206). Its short and round skull is joined to the spine (backbone), which supports the body. Vertebrae (the bones of the spine) protect the spinal cord, which is the main nerve cable in the body. The ribs are joined to the spine, forming a cage that protects a cat's heart and lungs. Cats' teeth are designed for killing and chewing meat. Wild cats have to be very careful not to damage their teeth, because with broken teeth they would quickly die from starvation.

Spine

The number of tail vertebrae varies according to the species. Tigers have from 23 to 26, but cheetahs have 28.

A big, flexible rib cage has 13 ribs.

The bones of a cat's powerful hind legs are longer than the front leg bones.

▲ THE FRAME

The powerfully built skeleton of a tiger is similar to all cats' skeletons. Cats have short necks with seven compressed vertebrae. These help to streamline and balance the cat so that it can achieve greater speeds. All cats have slightly different shoulder bones. A cheetah has long shoulder bones to which sprinting muscles are attached. A leopard, however, has short shoulder bones and thicker, tree-climbing muscles.

◀ CANINES AND CARNASSIALS

A tiger reveals its fearsome teeth. Its long, curved canines are adapted to fit between the neck bones of its prey to break the spinal cord. Like all carnivores, cats have strong back teeth, called carnassials. These do most of the cutting by tearing off pieces of meat.

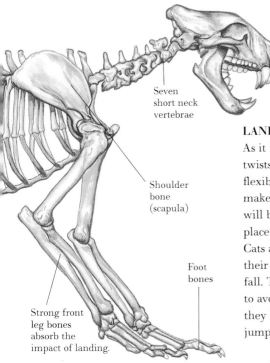

Seven
short neck
vertebrae

Shoulder
bone
(scapula)

Foot
bones

Strong front
leg bones
absorb the
impact of landing.

LANDING FEET ▶

As it falls, this cat
twists its supple,
flexible spine to
make sure its feet
will be in the right
place for landing.
Cats always land on
their feet when they
fall. This helps them
to avoid injury as
they leap on prey or
jump from a tree.

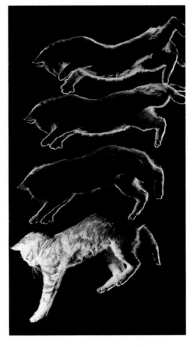

▼ CHEWING ON A BONE

Ravenous lions feast on the carcass of their latest
kill. Cats' jaws are hinged so that their jaw bones
can move only from side to side, not up and down.
Because of this, cats eat on one side of their mouths
at a time and often tilt their heads when they eat.

▼ CAT SKULL

Like all cats' skulls, this tiger's skull has a
high crown at the back giving lots of space
for its strong neck muscles. Big eye sockets
allow it to see well to the sides as well as to
the front. Its short jaws can open wide
to deliver a powerful bite.

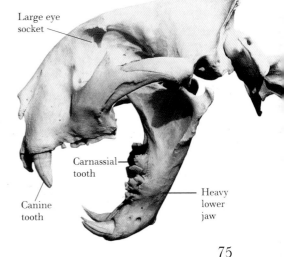

Large eye
socket

Carnassial
tooth

Canine
tooth

Heavy
lower
jaw

Muscles and Claws

Both inside and out, cats are designed to be skilled hunters and killers. Thick back and shoulder muscles help them to be excellent jumpers and climbers. Sharp, curved claws that grow from all of their digits (toes) are their weapons. One of the digits on a cat's front foot is called the dew claw. This is held off the ground to keep it sharp and ready to hold prey. Cats are warm-blooded, which means that their bodies stay at the same temperature no matter how hot or cold the weather is. The fur on their skin keeps them warm when conditions are cold. When it is hot, cats cool down by sweating through their noses and paw pads.

Heracles and the Nemean Lion
The mythical Greek hero Heracles was the son of the god Zeus and immensely strong. As a young man he committed a terrible crime. Part of his punishment was to kill the Nemean lion. The lion had impenetrable skin and could not be killed with arrows or spears. Heracles chased the lion into a cave and strangled it with his hands. He wore its skin as a shield and its head as a helmet.

▼ KNOCKOUT CLAWS

Cheetahs have well developed dew claws that stick out from the front legs. They use these claws to knock down prey before grabbing its throat or muzzle to strangle it. Other cats use their dew claws to grip while climbing or to hold on to prey. Cats have five claws, including the dew claw, on their front paws. On their back paws, they have only four claws.

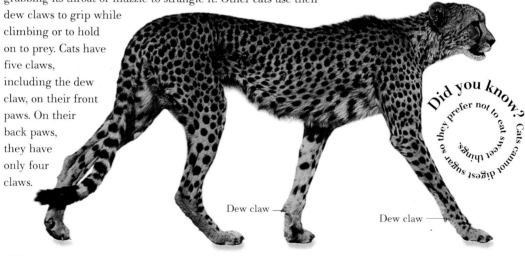

Did you know? Cats cannot digest sugar so they prefer not to eat sweet things.

Dew claw —

Dew claw —

Underneath the skin, a lion's muscular body follows the lines of its skeleton.

▲ TIGER CLAW

This is the extended claw of a tiger. Cats' claws are made of keratin, just like human fingernails. They need to be kept sharp all the time.

▲ MUSCLES FOR KILLING

Cats have very strong shoulder and neck muscles for attacking prey. The muscles also absorb some of the impact when the cat pounces.

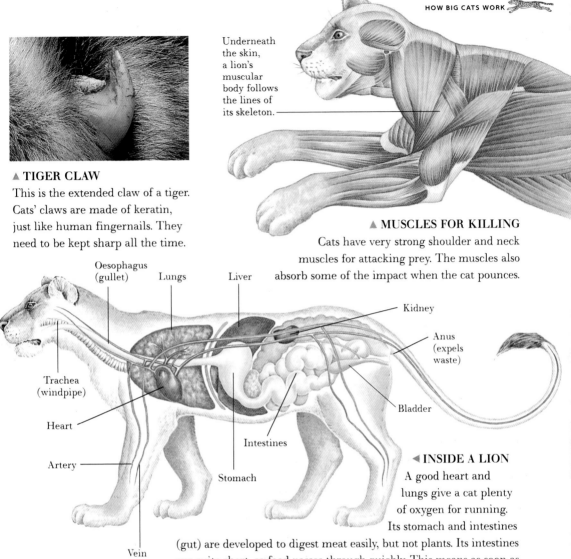

Oesophagus (gullet)

Lungs

Liver

Kidney

Anus (expels waste)

Trachea (windpipe)

Heart

Bladder

Artery

Intestines

Stomach

Vein

◀ INSIDE A LION

A good heart and lungs give a cat plenty of oxygen for running. Its stomach and intestines (gut) are developed to digest meat easily, but not plants. Its intestines are quite short, so food passes through quickly. This means as soon as it needs more food, a cat is light enough to run and pounce. Once a lion has had a big meal, it does not need to eat again for several days.

Flexed muscle

CLAW PROTECTION ▶

Cats retract (pull back) their claws into fleshy sheaths to protect them. This stops them getting blunt or damaged. Only cheetahs do not have sheaths.

Sheathed claw is protected by a fleshy covering.

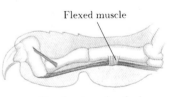

The claw is unsheathed when a muscle tightens.

77

Sight and Sound

To hunt well and not be seen or heard by prey or enemies, cats use their senses of sight, hearing and touch. Cats' eyesight is excellent. Their eyes are adapted for night vision, but they can also see well in the day. Cats' eyes are big compared to the size of their heads. They have good binocular vision, which allows them to accurately judge how far away objects are. At night, cats see in black and white. They can see colours in the day, but not as well as humans can. Cats have very good hearing, much better than a human's. They can hear small animals rustling through the grass or even moving around in their burrows underground.

Did you know? A cat's pupils open wide when it is frightened and close up when angry.

▲ **CAUGHT IN BRIGHT LIGHT**
Cats' eyes are very sensitive to light. During the day in bright light, the pupils of the eyes close right down, letting in only as much light as is needed to see well. A domestic cat's pupils close down to slits, while most big cats' pupils close to tiny circles.

◀ **GLOWING EYES**
Behind the retinas (light sensitive areas) in this leopard's eyes is a reflecting layer called the tapetum lucidum. This helps to absorb extra light in the dark. When light shines into the eyes at night the reflectors glow.

PREY IN SIGHT ▷

As it stalks through the long grass a lion must pounce at just the right moment if it is to catch its prey. Binocular vision helps the cat to judge when to strike. Because its eyes are set slightly apart at the front of the head their field of view overlaps. This enables a cat to judge the position of its prey exactly.

▲ ROUND-EYED

This puma's rounded pupils have closed down in daylight. In dim light, the pupils will expand wide to let in as much light as possible.

Large earflaps concentrate sound waves deep into each ear.

SHARP EARS ▷

Cats' ears are designed for them to hear very well. This Siberian lynx lives in snowy forests where the sound is soft and muffled. It has specially shaped, big ears to catch as much sound as possible.

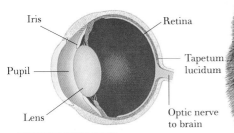

Iris

Retina

Pupil

Tapetum lucidum

Lens

Optic nerve to brain

▲ INSIDE THE EYE

The lens focuses light rays to produce a sharp image on the retina. Impulses from the retina are carried to the brain by the optic nerve. Cats have a membrane that can be pulled over the surface of the eye to keep out dirt and dust.

Touching, Tasting, Smelling

Like all animals, cats feel things with nerves in their skin, but they have another important touching tool – whiskers. These long, stiff hairs on the face have very sensitive nerve endings at their roots. Some whiskers are for protection. Anything brushing against the whiskers above a cat's eyes will make it blink. Cats use smell and taste to communicate with each other. A cat's tongue is a useful tool and its nose is very sensitive. Thin, curled bones in the nose carry scents inwards to smell receptors. Unlike most animals, cats have a special place on the roof of their mouth to taste smells, especially the scent of other cats.

▲ TONGUE TOOL
A leopard curls the tip of its tongue like a spoon to lap up water. After several laps it will drink the water in one gulp. As well as drinking, the tongue is used for tasting, scraping meat off a carcass and grooming.

◀ ROUGH TONGUE
A tiger's bright pink tongue has a very rough surface. Cats' tongues are covered with small spikes called papillae. The papillae point backwards and are used by the cat, together with its teeth, to strip meat off bones. Around the edge and at the back of the tongue are taste buds. Cats cannot taste sweet things, but can actively recognize pure water.

The tiger raises its head and grimaces to taste the air.

Cats twitch their tails from side to side as they concentrate. When angry, the tail lashes to and fro.

WHO PASSED BY? ▷

By tasting the air a tiger uses his Jacobson's organ (the special scent centre on the roof of the mouth) to detect the scent left by another tiger. To get as much of the scent as he can, he wrinkles his nose, curls his lips upwards, bares his teeth and lifts his head. This action is known as flehmen. Males use it especially to locate females ready to mate.

Did you know? Hairballs coughed up by lions are worn as talismans in parts of Africa.

▲ THE CAT'S WHISKERS

This snow leopard's face is surrounded by sensitive whiskers. Cats use their whiskers to judge how far away objects are. The most important whiskers are on the sides of the face. These help a cat to feel its way in the dark, or when it is walking through tall grass.

▼ COAT CARE

The long, rough tongue of a lion makes a very good comb. It removes loose hairs and combs the fur flat and straight. Cats wipe their faces, coats and paws clean. They need to keep well groomed and spend a lot of time looking after their fur. Hair swallowed by grooming is spat out as hairballs.

Spots and Stripes

A cat's fur coat protects its skin and keeps it warm. The coat's colours and patterns help to camouflage (hide) the cat as it hunts prey. Wild cats' coats have two layers – an undercoat of short soft fur and an outercoat of tougher, longer hairs, called guard hairs. Together these two layers insulate the cat from extreme cold or extreme heat. Some guard hairs are sensitive and help a cat to feel its way. Cats have loose skin, making it difficult for an attacker to get a good grip and helping to prevent injury. The colours and patterns of a wild cat's coat depend on where it lives.

▲ **TIGER IN THE GRASS**
The stripes of a tiger's coat are the perfect camouflage for an animal that needs to prowl around in long grass. The colours and patterns help to make the cat almost invisible as it stalks its prey. These markings are also very effective in a leafy jungle where the dappled light makes stripes of light and shade.

Did you know? Domestic cats have a wider range of colours and markings than wild cats.

◀ **KING OF THE HILL**
King cheetahs were once thought to be different from other cheetahs. They have longer fur, darker colours and spots on their backs that join up to form stripes. Even so, they are the same species. All cheetahs have distinctive tear stripes running from the corners of their eyes down beside their muzzles.

▲ NON-IDENTICAL TWINS

Many big cats of the same species come in variations of colour, depending on where they live. These two leopard cubs are twins, but one has a much darker, blackish coat. Black leopards are called panthers. (Black jaguars and pumas are also sometimes called panthers.) Some leopards live deep in the shadows of the forest, where a darker colouring would allow them to hide more easily. Panthers are most common in Asia.

▼ SPOT THE DIFFERENCE

Spots, stripes or blotches break up the outline of a cat's body. This helps it to blend in with the shadows made by the leaves of bushes and trees, or the lines of tall grass. In the dappled light of a forest or in the long grass of the savanna, cats are very well hidden indeed.

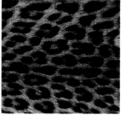
A leopard's spots are in fact small rosettes.

The tiger has distinctive black stripes.

A jaguar has rosettes with a central spot of colour.

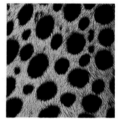
The cheetah has lots of spots and no rosettes.

◄ WHITE FOR SNOW

A snow leopard has a shaggy, off-white coat with darker spots. This colouring helps the snow leopard to stay well hidden in the rocky, mountainous terrain where it lives. It moves about early in the morning or late afternoon, blending with its habitat as it looks for prey.

A snow leopard's pale, thick coat has dark irregular spots and streaks. This helps it hide between the rocks and snow.

83

On the Move

Cats run and jump easily and gracefully. They have
flexible spines and long, strong hind legs.
With long, bouncy strides, they can cover a
lot of ground very quickly. Big cats are
not good long-distance runners, they
are sprinters and pouncers. They use
their long tails for balance when
climbing trees and running fast. All
cats can swim very well, but some do
not like the water and will only
swim to escape danger. Others,
such as tigers and jaguars, live
near water and often
swim to hunt
their prey.

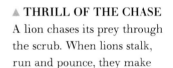

▲ THRILL OF THE CHASE
A lion chases its prey through
the scrub. When lions stalk,
run and pounce, they make
use of their flexible backs, strong back legs,
powerful chests and cushioning pads under their
paws. Cats' back legs are especially powerful.
They provide the major thrust for running. Cats
can outpace their prey over short distances
before launching into a final jump.

◀ TREE-CLIMBING CAT
Leopards spend a lot of time in trees
and are designed for climbing. They
have very powerful chests and front
legs. Their shoulder blades are
positioned to the side to
make them better climbers.
A leopard can leap 3m without
difficulty and, in exceptional
circumstances, can leap over 6m.

84

◄ SOFT PADDING

The thick pads under a lion's paw are like cushions. They allow the lion to move very quietly and also act as shock absorbers for running and jumping. Hidden between the pads and fur are the lion's claws, tucked away safely until they are needed.

GRACE AND AGILITY ►

A bobcat leaps with great agility off a rock. All cats have flexible backs and short collar bones to help make their bodies stronger for jumping off things. Bobcats are similar to lynxes. Both cats have an extensive coating of fur on their feet to give them extra warmth. The fur also prevents them from slipping on icy rocks.

Did you know? In the 1500s, rich people kept cheetahs as hunting animals like dogs.

As it leaps, a bobcat pinpoints its landing position. The front feet land separately in quick succession.

◄ KEEPING COOL CAT

A Bengal tiger swims gracefully across a river. Many tigers live in warm climates, such as India and Southeast Asia. As well as swimming to get from one place to another, they often look for pools of water to bathe in during the heat of the day. They are one of the few cats that actively enjoy being in or near water. Tigers are excellent swimmers and can easily cross a lake 5km wide.

Focus on the

A cheetah can run at 115km per hour over short distances — a speed equivalent to a fast car. This makes it the world's fastest land animal. The cheetah's body is fine-tuned for speed. It has wide nostrils to breathe in as much oxygen as possible and specially adapted paws for running fast. Most cheetahs today live in east and southern Africa, with a small number living in Asia — in Iran and Pakistan. They live in many different kinds of habitats, from open grassland to thick bush and even in desert-like environments.

1 A pair of cheetahs creep up stealthily on a herd of antelope. Cheetahs hunt their prey by slinking towards the herd, holding their heads low. Cheetahs are not pouncing killers, like other cats. Instead, they pull down their prey after a very fast chase. In order to waste as little energy as possible, cheetahs plan their attack first. They pick out their target before starting the chase.

2 The cheetah begins its chase as the herd of antelope starts to move. It can accelerate from walking pace to around 70km per hour in two seconds. Cheetahs have retractable claws, but unlike other cats they have no protective sheaths. The uncovered claws act like the spikes on the bottom of track shoes, helping the cheetah to grip as it runs. Ridges on their paw pads also help to improve grip.

3 At top speed a cheetah makes full use of its flexible spine and lean, supple body. A cheetah's legs are very long and slender compared to its body. It can cover several metres in a single bound.

Hunting Cheetah

4 As the cheetah closes in on the herd, the antelope spring in all directions. The cheetah changes direction without slowing down. If a cheetah does not catch its prey within about 400m, it has to give up the chase. Cheetahs usually hunt in the morning or late in the afternoon, when it is not too hot. They have short lifespans in the wild, because their speed declines with age.

5 As the cheetah closes in on its prey it may have to make several sharp turns to keep up. The cheetah's long tail gives it excellent balance as it turns. The cheetah knocks its victim off balance with a swipe of its front paw. It uses its big dew claw to pull the victim to the ground.

6 Once the prey animal is down, the cheetah grabs the victim's throat. A sharp bite suffocates the antelope. Cheetahs are not strong enough to kill by biting through the spinal cord in the prey's neck like other cats. The cheetah will hang on to the victim's throat until the antelope is dead.

Communication

All big cats communicate with one another. They tell each other how old they are, whether they are male or female, what mood they are in and where they live. Cats communicate by signals such as smells, scratches and sounds. The smells come from urine and from scent glands. Cats have scent glands on their heads and chins, between their toes and at the base of their tails. Every time they rub against something, they transfer their special smell. Cats make many different sounds. Scientists know that cats speak to each other, but still do not understand much about their language. Cats also communicate using body language. They use their ears to signal their mood and twitch their tails to show if they are excited or agitated.

▲ A MIGHTY ROAR

The lion's roar is the loudest sound cats make. It is loud enough for all the neighbourhood lions to hear. Lions roar after sunset, following a kill and when they have finished eating. Lions make at least nine different sounds. They also grunt to each other as they move around.

HISSING LEOPARD ▶

An angry leopard hisses at an enemy. Cats hiss and spit when they feel threatened, or when they are fighting an enemy. The position of a cat's ears also signals its intentions. When a cat is about to attack, it flattens its ears back against its neck.

▲ EAR SIGNALS

Many wild cats, such as this tiger, have white markings on the back of their ears. They turn their ears to show the markings to an enemy when they are angry.

▲ MARKS FOR SHOW

Cats like to scratch things to clean their claws and stretch their limbs. At the same time they leave a scented mark for others to both see and smell. When this lioness scratches, she leaves her own personal scent from the glands between her toes on the scratch marks.

▲ CAT SPRAY

A king cheetah marks its territory by spraying urine at points along its trails. Scent marks left by a male tell other males to keep away. The scent left by a female will tell a male passing through her range if she is ready to mate.

BABY TALK ▶

Mothers talk to their cubs a lot. The sounds are quiet so that enemies do not hear. The softest and safest sound of all is purring.

Did you know? When they are close together, lions chirrup, meow and yowl to each other.

Hunting Prey

All cats, big and small, are carnivores – they eat meat. Their bodies are not designed to digest plants. Big cats must hunt down and kill their own food. Most big cats, however, are only too happy to eat someone else's meal and steal kills from other animals whenever they can. Cheetahs are an exception, and eat only animals they have killed themselves. To catch and kill their food, big cats must hunt. Some, like cheetahs, patrol their neighbourhoods, looking for prey. Others, such as jaguars, hide in wait and then ambush their victims. Many cats, such as leopards, do both.

King Solomon
Solomon ruled Israel in the 900s BC and was reputed to be a very wise ruler. His throne was carved with lions because of his admiration for these big cats who killed only out of necessity. In law, if a man was said to have fallen into a lions' den, it was not proof of his death

◀ THE MAIN COURSE
A big lion can kill large, powerful animals like this buffalo. A big cat usually attacks from behind, or from the side. If the prey is too big to grab straight away, the cat will knock it off balance, hold on to it and bite into its neck.

CHOOSING A MEAL ▶
A herd of antelope and zebra graze while keeping watch on a lioness crouched in the grass. She lies as close to the ground as possible, waiting to pounce. Finally, when focused on a victim, she will bring her hind legs back into position and dart forwards.

▲ WARTHOG SPECIAL

Four cheetahs surround an injured warthog. The mother cheetah is teaching her three cubs hunting techniques. The cheetah on the right is trying a left paw side swipe, while another tries using its dew claw. Cheetahs love to eat warthogs but also catch antelope and smaller animals such as hares.

▲ CAT AND MOUSE

A recently killed capybara (a large rodent) makes a tasty meal for a jaguar. Jaguars often catch their food in water, such as fish and turtles. On land they hunt armadillos, deer, opossums, skunks, snakes, squirrels, tortoises and monkeys.

Did you know? Cheetahs will only chase prey if it runs. If it stops, so does the cheetah.

SLOW FOOD ▶

If a lion has not been able to hunt successfully for a while, it will eat small creatures such as this tortoise. Lions usually hunt big animals such as antelope, wildebeest, warthogs, giraffe, buffalo, bush pigs and baboons. They work together in a group to hunt large prey.

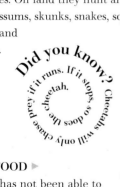

Killing Prey

The way a big cat kills its prey depends on the size of the cat and the size of its meal. If the prey is small with a bite-sized neck, it will be killed with a bite through the spinal cord. If the prey has a bite-sized head, the cat will use its powerful jaws to crush the back of its skull. Large prey is killed by biting its throat and suffocating it. Lions often hunt together and use a combined effort to kill large prey. One lion may grab the prey's nose to suffocate it, while other lions attack from behind.

Did you know? Lions try to flip porcupines on to their backs to avoid the sharp spines.

▼ **OLD AGE**
When big cats get old or injured it is very difficult for them to hunt. They will eventually die from starvation. This lion from the Kalahari Desert in South Africa is old and thin. It has been weakened by hunger.

◀ **FAIR GAME**
A warthog is a small, delicious meal for a cheetah. The bigger the cat, the bigger its prey. A cheetah is quite a light cat, so to kill an animal the cheetah first knocks it over, then bites the prey's neck to suffocate it.

▲ **A DEADLY EMBRACE**
A lioness immobilizes a struggling wildebeest by biting its windpipe and suffocating it to death. Lions are very strong animals. A lion weighing 150 to 250kg can kill a buffalo more than twice its weight. Female lions do most of the hunting for their pride.

◀ SECRET STASH

A cheetah carrying off its prey, a young gazelle, to a safe place. Once it has killed, a cheetah will check the area to be sure it is secure before feeding. It drags the carcass to a covered spot in the bushes. Here it can eat its meal hidden from enemies. Cheetahs are often driven off and robbed of their kills by hyenas and jackals or even other big cats.

A SOLID MEAL ▶

These cheetahs will devour as much of this antelope as they can. Big cats lie on the ground and hold their food with their forepaws when they eat. When they have satisfied their hunger, cheetahs cover up or hide the carcass with grass, leaves or whatever is available in order to save it for later.

LIONS' FEAST ▶

A pride of lions gather around their kill, a zebra. They eat quickly before any scavenging hyenas and vultures can steal the meat. Each lion has its place in the pride. Even if they are very hungry, they must wait until it is their turn to eat. Usually the dominant male lion eats first.

Focus on the Lone

Leopards are one of the most widespread of all the big cats, but are also the most secretive. They live in many different habitats throughout Africa and southern Asia, in open, rocky country as well as forests. Not much is known about them because they are nocturnal animals, coming out to hunt at night. They sometimes creep up on prey on the ground, then pounce. At other times they ambush their quarry from a tree.

CAT NAP

Leopards usually sleep all day in a tree, especially when it is very hot. Their spotted coat is excellent camouflage in the patchwork of light and shade in the forest. It is so good that, when they are resting, they are especially hard to see.

LONE LEOPARD

Leopards are loners. They come together only when a female signals to a male that she is ready to mate. After mating they separate again. The mother brings up the cubs until they are able to fend for themselves.

Leopard

BRUTE STRENGTH
A leopard drags its dead victim across the ground. Leopards have strong jaws, chests and front legs so that they can move an animal as big as themselves.

AMBUSH
Leopards like to ambush prey. They climb on to a low branch and wait for an animal to walk underneath. Then they jump down and grab it. The leopard uses its great strength to drag its victim high up into the tree. Prey includes pigs, antelope, monkeys, dogs and many other animals.

TOP MEAL
This leopard has dragged its kill up into a tree. This is to prevent the carcass being stolen. Other big carnivores that live in the same area cannot climb trees as well as leopards. Once the prey is safe, a leopard can finish its meal.

95

Living Together

Most big cats live alone. They hunt alone and the females bring up their cubs alone. Big cats come together only when they want to mate. They are solitary because of the prey that they hunt. There is usually not enough prey in one area for a large group of big cats to live on. Lions are the exception. They live in family groups called prides. (Male cheetahs also sometimes live in groups with up to four members.) All wild cats have territories (home ranges). These territories are a series of trails that link together a cat's hunting area, its drinking places, its lookout positions and the den where it brings up its young. Females have smaller home ranges than males. Males that have more than one mate have territories that overlap with two or more female home ranges.

Did you know? Big cats' territories range from a few kilometres to over 1,000 km.

▲ BRINGING UP BABY

Female snow leopards bring up their cubs on their own. They have up to five cubs who stay with their mother for at least a year. Although snow leopards are loners, they are not unsociable. They like to live near each other and let other snow leopards cross their territories.

◀ THE LOOKOUT

A puma keeps watch over its territory from a hill. Pumas are solitary and deliberately avoid each other except during courtship and mating. The first male puma to arrive in an area claims it as his territory. He chases out any other male that tries to live there.

▲ A PRIDE OF LIONS

The lions in a pride drink together, hunt together, eat together and play together. A pride is usually made up of related females and their young. Prides usually try not to meet up with other prides. To tell the others to keep out of their territory, the pride leaves scent markings on the edge of their range.

Daniel and the Lions' Den

A story in the Bible tells how Daniel was taken prisoner by Nebuchadnezzer, king of Babylon. When Daniel correctly interpreted the king's dreams he became a favourite of the king. His enemies became jealous of his position and had him thrown into a lions' den, a common punishment for prisoners at the time. But instead of eating Daniel, the lions befriended him. They were tamed by his great faith in God.

▲ FAMILY GROUPS

A cheetah mother sits between her two cubs. The cubs will stay with her until they are about 18 months old. The female then lives a solitary life. Males, however, live in small groups and defend a territory. They only leave their range if there is a drought or if food is very scarce.

▲ WELL GROOMED

Cats that live together groom each other. They do this to be friendly and to keep clean. They also groom to spread their scent on each other, so that they smell the same. This helps them to recognize each other and to identify strangers.

97

Focus on

Lions are the second largest of the big cats after tigers. They like to live in open spaces, sometimes in woodland, but never in tropical forests. Lions are usually found on the savanna (grassy plains) and on the edges of deserts. Female lions live together in prides (family groups) of up to 12 lionesses and their cubs. The size of the group depends on how much food there is available. Male lions may live together in groups, called coalitions, which look after one or more prides. The coalitions defend their prides, fighting off any other males who want to mate with the females of their pride.

FATHER AND SON

Male lions are the only big cats that look different from the females. They have long shaggy manes to look larger and fiercer and to protect their necks in a fight.
A male cub starts to grow a mane at about the age of three. At that age he also leaves the pride to establish his own territory.

THE FAMILY

A pride of lions rests near a waterhole. The biggest prides live in open grasslands where there are large herds of antelope, wildebeest and buffalo. If a foreign male takes over a pride, the new lion kills all the cubs under six months old. This is to ensure all the cubs are his.

a Pride

NURSERY SCHOOL
Young lions play tag to learn how to chase things and to defend their pride. The pride does not usually allow strange lions to join the family group. Young lions need to be prepared in case other lions come to fight with them.

FIRST AT THE TABLE
Male lions usually eat first, even though the females do most of the hunting. He can eat up to 30kg of meat at one time, but he will not need to eat again for several days.

CAT SCRAP
Two lionesses fight each other to decide who will be top cat. There is usually a dominant female in each pride, even when there are males around. This chief female rules the family.

MOTHER AND CUBS
Lionesses give birth to a litter of between one and six cubs. The cubs start learning to hunt when they are about 11 months old, but stay with their mother for over two years. In dry areas, lions live in small prides because less food is available.

Lionesses help to raise the young together. They even suckle each other's cubs.

Finding a Mate

Big cats roam over large areas, so it can be quite difficult for them to find a partner. When they are ready to mate, they use scent markers. These are like advertisements to all the other cats in the district. A  female also calls loudly, in the hope that a nearby male will come to her. Often more than one male will follow a female. This almost always leads to fights between the interested males. The winner of the fight then begins to court the female. In a pride of lions, one male establishes his dominance over the group. In this way he avoids having to fight every time a female is ready to mate. Many big cats will mate several times a day for up to a week to make sure that the female is pregnant.

▲ SIGNS OF LOVE

A male lion rubs against a female and smells her all over. He knows that the lioness is ready to mate from her scent. Having fought off rivals, he must now persuade the lioness to mate with him. He courts her by being attentive. Their courtship may last for several days before they mate.

Did you know?
Pumas are also called mountain screamers after the female's mating call.

◄ THE HAPPY COUPLE

When the female is ready to mate, she crouches on the ground with her hindquarters slightly raised. The male sits behind and over her and sometimes holds the scruff of her neck between his jaws. Large cats, such as leopards and lions, may mate up to 100 times a day. Smaller cats, such as cheetahs, are more vulnerable to predators and so mate for a shorter time.

KEEPING HIM IN HIS PLACE ▶

After mating the lioness is aggressive and often lashes out at the lion. As soon as the two have mated the male jumps back very quickly. He remains close by her side to stop other males approaching. Once she has calmed down she rolls on her back and they mate again. Each mating lasts only a few seconds.

Did you know? A wild big cat may have up to 5 litters in an average lifespan of 12 years.

▲ LEAN AND HEALTHY

This lioness is only just pregnant. She has not put on much weight and can still hunt efficiently. At the end of her pregnancy (about three to four months long) she will hunt small, easy-to-catch prey. Lionesses in a pride also get to share in the pride's kill.

▼ CAT ATTRACTION

Two courting tigers often make a great deal of noise. They roar, meow, moan and grunt as they mate. Female tigers mate every other year. The male stays close by the female for a few days until he is sure she is pregnant. Then the pair separate and live on their own again.

Giving Birth

The cubs (babies) of a big cat are usually born with spotted fur and closed eyes. They are completely helpless. The mother cat looks after them on her own with no help from the father. She gives birth in a safe place called a den. For the first few days after birth, she stays very close to her cubs so that they can feed on her milk. She keeps them warm and cleans the cubs by licking them all over. The cubs grow quickly. Even before their eyes open they can crawl, and they soon learn to hiss to defend themselves.

▲ SNOW CUB

Snow leopard cubs have white fur with dark spots. They are always born in the spring and open their eyes one week after birth. The cubs begin to follow their mothers around when they are about three months old. By winter, they will be almost grown up.

MOTHERLY LOVE ▶

Tiger cubs are capable killers by the time they are 11 months old. They stay with their mothers, however, until they are two or even three years of age. In the wild, the mother does all she can to protect her young, but often at least half of the litter dies. Predators may kill the cubs, or sometimes they starve to death if the mother cannot catch enough food.

IN DISGUISE ▶

A cheetah cub is covered in long, woolly fur. This makes it look similar to the African honey badger, a very fierce animal, which may help to discourage predators. The mother cheetah does not raise her cubs in a den, but moves them around every few days.

A cheetah cub, unlike the adult, has a mane of fur. This may help to disguise it as it hides in the long grass.

▲ BRINGING UP BABY

Female pumas give birth to up to six kittens (babies). The mother has several pairs of teats for the kittens to suckle from. Each kitten has its own teat and will use no other. They will suckle her milk for at least three months and from about six weeks they will also eat meat.

▲ ON GUARD

Two lionesses guard the entrance to their den. Lions are social cats and share the responsibility of keeping guard. Dens are kept very clean so that there are no smells to attract predators.

▲ MOVING TO SAFETY

If at any time a mother cat thinks her cubs are in danger, she will move them to a new den. She carries the cubs one by one, gently grasping the loose skin at their necks between her teeth.

103

Focus on

The number of cubs in a big cat's litter depends on the species and where it lives. Most big cats have two or three cubs, but cheetahs have five or more. All cubs are born helpless, but it is not long before their eyes open and they can wobble about, learning to balance on their uncertain legs. Within a few weeks they begin to play with their mothers and each other. There is a lot to find out, but they learn very quickly. By the time they are six months old they will have learned how to keep safe, what food tastes good and how to catch it. They will start to understand the language of smells and sounds. For the next year and a half they will stay close to their mothers, practising their new skills until they are experts.

PLAY TIME
A cub plays with its mother's tail. As soon as cubs can see, they begin to play. Play helps to build up muscles, improve co-ordination and develop good reflexes. It is valuable early preparation for learning how to hunt when the cubs are older.

SAFETY FIRST
For the first two years of their lives, cubs remain close to their mother. She protects them and helps them when they make mistakes. A good mother may rear all her cubs successfully in a good year. A poor mother may lose most or even all of her cubs.

BATH TIME
Cubs must learn to clean themselves, but while they are still young their mother washes them with her tongue. As she licks, she spreads her scent on the cubs so that all of her family has the same smell.

Cute Cubs

FAMILY BLISS

Lion cubs are spotted all over to help hide them from predators. The spots gradually fade as the lions grow older. Adult lions have only very faint spots on their legs and stomachs. Lion cubs are lucky because they have many companions to play with. Cubs of solitary cats have to grow up without much company. Some do not even have any brothers or sisters. Lion cubs learn through play how to get on with their fellows.

MOVING HOME

To move her cubs a lioness carries each one gently in her mouth. Not only do the cubs have loose skin at their necks, but the lioness has a special gap in her mouth behind the canines. This allows her to lift the cub off the ground without biting it.

LION LESSONS

These cubs are working together to kill an injured warthog. One grabs the neck, while the other starts tearing at the hind leg. The mother lioness watches over them. She is the cubs' teacher. They must learn to hunt as soon as possible and this warthog is a small animal for them to begin with. The lioness brought down the warthog so that the cubs could learn to kill it.

Growing Up

Growing cubs have to learn all about life as an adult so that they can look after themselves when they leave their mother. She teaches them as much as she can and the rest they learn through play. Cub games depend on their species, because each type of cat has different things to learn. In play-fighting cheetahs use their paws to knock each other over. This is a technique they will need for hunting when they are older. Cubs need to learn how to judge distances and when to strike to kill prey quickly, without getting injured or killed themselves. Their mother introduces them to prey by bringing an animal back to the den to eat. Mothers and cubs use very high-pitched sounds to communicate. If she senses danger, she growls at them to tell them to hide.

▲ **PRACTICE MAKES PERFECT**
These cheetah cubs are learning to kill a Thomson's gazelle. When the cubs are about 12 weeks old, a mother cheetah brings back live injured prey for them to kill. They instinctively know how to do so, but need practice to get it right.

▼ **FOLLOW MY LEADER**
Curious cheetah cubs watch an object intently, safe beside their mother. At about six weeks the cubs start to go on hunting trips with her. They are able to keep up by following her white-tipped tail through the tall grass.

THE CLASSROOM ▷

A group of lion cubs relax in the shade on a fallen tree. From here they watch the adults hunt, as if in a big, open-air classroom. Female cubs often stay in the pride, but young males are chased off by the dominant male.

◁ SCRATCH AND SNIFF

Three young lions sniff at the shell of a tortoise. Cubs learn to be cautious when dealing with unfamiliar objects. First the object is tapped with a paw, before being explored further with the nose. Cubs' milk teeth are replaced with permanent canine teeth at about two years old. Not until then can they begin to hunt and kill big animals.

TAIL TOY ▷

A mother leopard's tail is a good thing for her cub to learn to pounce on. She twitches it so the cub can develop good co-ordination and timing. As the cub grows, it will practise on rodents and then bigger animals until it can hunt for itself. Once they leave their mothers, female cubs usually establish a territory close by, while males go farther away.

107

Enemies of Big Cats

Big cats are perfect killing machines and are feared by all their prey. They do, however, have enemies. Big cats have to watch out for other carnivores taking their food or attacking their cubs. Wolves are a problem for pumas; wild dogs are a threat to tigers; hyenas and jackals prey on the cubs of African big cats. Even prey animals can be a danger to big cats. Buffaloes are very aggressive and can attack and kill a young lion. Humans, however, are the main enemies of wild cats. As people move farther into the wilderness to build homes and farms, they destroy the precious habitats of the big cats. People kill the big cats' prey, leaving them with less to eat. They also hunt big cats for their beautiful and valuable fur coats.

▲ **SCAVENGING HYENAS**
A spotted hyena finishes off the remains of a giraffe. Hyenas live in Africa and western Asia. They eat whatever they can find. This is often carrion (the remains of dead prey) that animals such as big cats have killed for themselves. They will also kill cubs. Hyenas have strong jaws and bone-crunching teeth and look for food at night.

Did you know? Despite their dog-like appearance, hyenas are more closely related to cats.

◀ **PACK POWER**
Wolves live in Europe and North America. They live in the mountains as well as on open plains, hunting in packs of up to 20 animals. Wolves usually eat deer, elk, moose, or small animals such as hares. But they never ignore a good meal caught by a puma.

BIG CAT THREAT ▶

Leopards live in the same areas as cheetahs, but they are very hostile towards them. In fact, if they get a chance, leopards prey on cheetahs and their cubs. In turn, leopards have to be very wary of lions. Lions will attack and kill a leopard to protect the pride or their territory. Big cats do not like others because of competition for food in an area.

▲ HUMAN TRAPS

Experts examine a tiger trap. Poachers (people who kill animals illegally) often use traps to catch big cats. When the trap snaps shut, the animal is stuck until it dies or until the poacher returns to kill it. These traps cause great pain. A cat may try to chew off its trapped leg to escape.

▼ DOG-LIKE JACKALS

Jackals (a relative of the dog) are half the size of hyenas and live in Africa. They will eat most things and will steal a big cat's kill. If they come across an unprotected den, they quickly kill and eat all the cubs.

◀ INTRUDER PERIL

Sometimes big cats become cannibals and eat their own kind. These cheetahs are eating another cheetah that has invaded their territory. Male lions also eat all the young cubs in a pride when they take over dominance from another male.

109

Mountain Cats

To live in the mountains, cats need to be hardy and excellent rock climbers. They also have to cope with high altitudes where the air is thin and there is less oxygen to breathe. Big cats that live in the mountains include leopards and the rare snow leopard. Small cats include the puma, mountain cat, bobcat and lynx. Mountain climates are harsh and the weather can change very quickly. To survive, mountain cats need to use their wits and to know where to find shelter. They mate so that their cubs are born in the spring. This is to ensure that they will be almost grown by the time winter closes in.

▲ **MOUNTAIN CAT**
The mountain cat is a secretive, shy creature and seldom seen. It is about 50cm long and has soft, fine fur. It is also known as the Andean mountain cat, since it lives in the high Andes mountains of Chile, Argentina, Peru and Bolivia. This cat is found at altitudes of up to 5,000m above sea level.

This map shows the world's major mountain ranges. The puma, mountain cat and lynx live in the Americas. Lynx also live in Europe and Asia, while the snow leopard lives in Asia.

◀ **MOUNTAIN LION**
A puma keeps watch over its vast territory. Pumas are also known as mountain lions and cougars. Male pumas can grow to 2m long and weigh 100kg. They are good at jumping and can easily leap 5m on to a high rock or into a tree. Pumas are found over a wide area, from Canada to the very tip of South America. They live along the foothills of mountains, in forests on mountain slopes and all the way up to 4,500m above sea level. Depending on where they live, pumas will eat deer, porcupines, hares, beavers and armadillos.

WINTER LYNX ▶

Lynx live in mountainous regions of Europe. Asia and North America. They have unusually short tails and tufted ears. Lynx are well designed to live in very cold places. In winter they grow an especially long coat, which is light coloured so that they are well camouflaged in the snow. The bobcat of North America looks similar to the lynx.

◀ PUMA CHASE

A snowshoe hare darts this way and that to shake off a puma. To catch the hare, the puma must make full use of its flexible back and its long balancing tail. Pumas hunt by day as well as by night.

LONG-TAILED SNOW LEOPARD ▶

The snow leopard is one of the rarest big cats, found only in the Himalaya and Altai mountains of central Asia. It can live at altitudes of 6,000m, the highest of any wild cat. Snow leopards feed on wild goats, hares and marmots. Their bodies measure just over 1m long, with tails that are almost as long. They wrap their bushy tails around themselves to keep warm when they are sleeping. Snow leopards are particularly agile jumpers and said to be able to leap a gap of 15m. Their long tails help them balance as they jump.

Did you know? A female snow leopard makes her den cosy by lining it with her own fur.

111

Forest Dwellers

Dense, wet rainforests are home to lots of small creatures, such as insects and spiders. These animals and forest plants provide a feast for birds, snakes, frogs and small mammals, which in turn are a banquet for big cats. Jaguars, tigers, leopards and clouded leopards all live in rainforests. Small cats include ocelots and margays. Although there is plenty of food in a forest, the dense trees make it a difficult place to hunt. There is little space among the trees and prey can escape easily in the thick undergrowth.

▲ **CLOUDED LEOPARD**
The clouded leopard is a shy and rarely seen Asian big cat. It lives in forests from Nepal to Borneo, spending most of its time in the trees. The Chinese call the clouded leopard the mint leopard because of its unusual leaf-like markings. Male clouded leopards reach about 1m long, with an equally long tail, and weigh about 30kg. They are perfectly built for tree climbing, with a long, bushy tail for balance and flexible ankle joints.

This map shows where the world's tropical rainforests are located. They lie in a band either side of the Equator.

JAGUAR ▶
Although jaguars live in grasslands and semi-deserts, they prefer the thick forests of South and Central America. They are the third largest big cat (after tigers and lions), growing to 2.4 m in length and weighing up to 120kg.

Did you know? The jaguar was the symbol of the Sun for the Maya of Central America.

The sleek margay is very striking in appearance, with beautifully marked fur and large eyes.

▲ SUMATRAN TIGER

A tiger walks stealthily into a jungle pool on the island of Sumatra. Tigers are good swimmers and a forest pool is a good place to hunt as well as to cool off from the tropical heat. Tigers often hide the carcasses of their prey in water or the dense undergrowth.

▲ MARGAY

Margays live in the tropical forests of Central and South America. They are the best of all cat climbers, with broad, soft feet and exceptionally flexible ankles and hind legs. They feed largely on birds and so need to be good at moving around in the tops of trees.

▲ JAVAN LEOPARD

At one time, many leopards lived in the tropical rainforests of Asia. But now, like this Javan leopard, they are endangered. They are threatened by over-hunting and the destruction of their forest habitat.

◀ BLACK JAGUAR

Forest jaguars are darker than their grassland cousins. Some can be black and are so well camouflaged that they can disappear in the shadows of their forest habitat.

▲ A TURTLE TREAT

A jaguar catches a river turtle in a pool. Jaguars are such good swimmers that they hunt some of their prey in water. They love to eat fish and turtles. Their jaws are powerful enough to crack open a turtle's shell like a nut. They have been known to kill cayman (a type of crocodile).

Focus on

Tigers are the largest of all the big cats and the largest of all the tigers is the Siberian tiger. An adult male can reach up to 2.6m long and weigh as much as 270kg. Siberian tigers live in the snow-covered forests of Siberia, which is part of Russia, and Manchuria in China. They are also sometimes known as Amur tigers. Although there is only one species of tiger, they can differ significantly in their appearance. Siberian tigers have a relatively pale coat with few stripes. Bengal tigers from India, however, have shorter fur and are more strikingly marked. As humans destroy more of their habitats, the number of tigers in the wild is declining dramatically. Today, there are only about 400 Siberian tigers left in the wild.

SOLITARY SIBERIAN
Siberian tigers live alone in huge territories of over 1,000km. They do not like to fight and try to avoid each other. A tiger will kill another if it invades its territory.

LUNCH TIME
A group of Siberian tigers devour a black ox. Despite being solitary animals, tigers do sometimes share food. The only other time they come together is to mate. Tigers have been known to roar when they have killed a big animal, just as lions will often roar when they have successfully caught their prey.

OPEN WIDE
A Siberian tiger shows its long, sharp canine teeth in a wide yawn. Canines are used to catch and kill prey. Tigers ambush prey and kill it by biting the neck or strangling.

Siberian Tigers

ICY TONIC

A mother shows her 18-month-old cub how to get water from melted ice. Tigers have up to four cubs in a litter, every other year. They stay with her for at least two years.

COURTING COUPLE

When a female is ready to mate, she sprays, roars and grunts to tell the male. When tigers want to be friendly, they blow sharply through their nostrils and mouths, rub their heads together and gently bite each other's necks.

A PALE ICE QUEEN

Siberian tigers like this female have a lot of white fur. This makes it more difficult for prey and enemies to see them in the snow. They are powerfully and heavily built, with bodies slung close to the ground.

On the Savanna

Savannas are open, flat areas of grassland. Apart from grasses, the main plants of the savanna are small bushes and clumps of trees. Savanna is the ideal habitat for big herds of grazing animals, such as antelope, zebra and buffalo. In Africa, these herds migrate for thousands of kilometres each year in search of fresh grass and water. They are followed by lions, cheetahs and leopards who prey on the herds. The savanna of South America is home to jaguars. Rodents, such as mice, gerbils and marmots also thrive on the savanna and these are a good food source for smaller cats, such as the serval.

This map shows where the world's savannas (tropical grasslands and dry woodlands) are located. The largest region of savanna lies in Africa.

▲ **LION IN THE GRASS**
A lion walks through the long, dry grass of the African savanna. Its sandy colouring perfectly matches its habitat. Lions hunt their quarry using the cover of grass. Often, only the tips of a lion's ears are seen as it slowly stalks its prey.

Did you know? Cats sleep longer than most other animals. Lions sleep for 20 hours a day.

◀ **CHEETAH ON THE LOOKOUT**
A cheetah stands on the top of a small mound on the Kenyan savanna. Cheetahs are perfectly adapted for life on the plains. The surrounding open, flat terrain lets them make the most of their ability to chase down prey. From its vantage point, a cheetah uses its excellent eyesight to search for prey. It also keeps watch for any other cheetahs who might have invaded its home range.

◀ VIEW FROM A BRANCH

Leopards like to live in areas of grassland where there are trees. Here they can sleep hidden during the heat of the day. They can also enjoy the afternoon breeze and avoid the insect pests that live in the grass below. Leopards also prefer to eat up in a tree, out of the reach of scavengers.

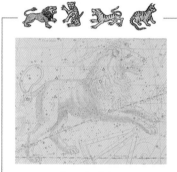

Leo the Lion
People born between July 24 and August 23 are born under the astrological sign of Leo (the lion). They are said to be brave, strong and proud, just like lions.

▲ AT THE WATERHOLE

During the dry season in the African savanna, many grazing animals gather near waterholes to drink. Thomson's gazelle, zebra and giraffe are shown here. Lions congregate around the waterholes, not only to drink, but also to catch prey unawares. Their favourite prey is antelope, buffalo, zebra and warthog, but they also eat giraffe.

SPEEDY SERVAL ▶

Servals are small cats that live on the savanna of western and central Africa. They like to live near water where there are bushes to hide in. The servals' long legs enable them to leap over tall grass when they hunt small rodents. They also climb well and hunt birds. With their long legs, servals can run quickly over short distances and so escape from predators.

117

Desert Cats

Hot deserts are very dry places. Although they are hot during the day, at night they are very cold. Few plants and animals can survive in such a harsh environment, but cats are very adaptable. Cheetahs, lions and leopards live in the Kalahari and Namib deserts of southern Africa. As long as there are animals to eat, the cats can survive. Even the jaguar, a cat that loves water, has been seen in desert areas in Mexico and the southern USA. But they are only visitors in this tough, dry land and soon go back to the wetter places they prefer. The most well-adapted cat to desert life is the sand cat. It lives in the northern Sahara Desert, the Middle East and western Asia.

Did you know? Lions follow along dry riverbeds looking for waterholes in the desert.

▲ **DESERT STORM**

Two lions endure a sandstorm in the Kalahari Desert of southern Africa. The desert is a very hostile place to live. There is very little water, not much food and the wind blows up terrible sandstorms. Despite these hardships, big cats like these lions manage to survive.

This map shows where the world's hot deserts and nearby semi-desert areas are located.

▼ **A HARSH LIFE**

An old lion drinks from a waterhole in the Kalahari Desert. Even when a big cat lives in a dry place, it still needs to find enough water to drink. This is often a difficult task, requiring the animals to walk long distances. In the desert, prey is usually very spread out, so an old lion has a hard time trying to feed itself adequately.

▲ CHEETAH WALK

A group of cheetahs walk across the wide expanse of the Kalahari Desert. They lead lives of feast and famine. In the rainy season, lush vegetation grows and enormous herds of antelope can graze. The cheetahs have a banquet preying on the grazing herds. But they go very hungry as the land dries up and prey becomes scarce.

Big ears hear the soft, high-pitched squeaks of rodents.

◀ SAND CAT

Dense hair on the soles of the sand cat's feet protect it as it walks on hot ground and help it walk on loose sand. All the water the cat needs comes from its food, so it does not need to drink.

Very thick, soft fur protects from the heat and cold.

▲ ADAPTABLE LEOPARD

A leopard rolls in the desert sand. There are very few trees in the desert, so leopards live among rocky outcrops. Here they can drag their prey to high places to eat in safety. The desert can be a dangerous place. With so little food around, competition can be fierce, especially with hungry lions. Big cats will eat small prey such as insects to keep off starvation.

Egyptian Cat Worship
The Ancient Egyptians kept cats to protect their stores of grain from rats and mice. Cats became so celebrated, they were worshipped as gods. They were sacred to the cat-headed goddess of pleasure, Bast. Many cats were given funerals when they died. Their bodies were preserved, wrapped in bandages and richly painted.

119

Killer Cats

Humans can sometimes become the prey of big cats. People have been afraid of big cats for thousands of years. From 20,000-year-old cave paintings we know that people lived in contact with big cats and almost certainly feared them. More recently, there have been many reports of big cats killing people. Lions and tigers become bold when they are hungry and there is little other food around. First they prey on livestock such as cattle. When the cattle are taken away, the big cats might kill people. Leopards, who do not have a natural fear of humans may have their killer instinct triggered by an injury.

▲ LION BAITING

The Romans used lions (and bears) for gladiator fights in their amphitheatres (outdoor arenas). When the Romans wanted to kill prisoners, they would feed them to hungry lions. The lions had to be starving and made angry by their handlers, otherwise they would not kill the prisoners. Most captive lions will not kill people.

◀ WRESTLING A TIGER

Tigers are considered the most dangerous of all the big cats. This picture, called *A Timely Rescue*, shows a rather heroic view of killing a tiger. Once a tiger has become used to the taste of human flesh, it will strike at any time. Tigers have killed thousands of people over the centuries. During the early 1900s, tigers killed 800 to 900 people a year in India.

Did you know? In the early 1900s, one Indian leopard killed 125 people in eight years.

▲ TIPPU'S TIGER

This mechanical toy of a tiger attacking a British soldier was made in 1790. It is called Tippu's Tiger and was made for the Sultan of Mysore. The Sultan resisted the British takeover of India and his toy makes growling and screaming noises.

◀ HUNTER WITH A HEART

Jim Corbett was a famous hunter who lived in India in the early 1900s. Unlike most hunters of his day, he did not kill big cats for sport. He shot tigers and leopards that had been eating people.

Jaguar Knights

In the 1500s in Central America, Aztec warriors were divided into military orders. Some of the most prestigious were the jaguar knights who ranked just below the emperor. They wore entire wild cats' pelts, with the still-attached heads worn as helmets. They thought by wearing the pelt they would take on the cat's strength and quiet stealth.

▲ EDUCATION FOR CONSERVATION

Nearly 100 tigers and 50 leopards live in the Corbett National Park in India. The Park runs programmes to teach children all about the big cats and their habitat. The more we know about big cats, the better able we are to respect them.

121

Cats in Danger

The earliest record that we have of people using wild-cat pelts (skins) is from 6,500BC. It comes from the archeological site of Çatal Hüyük in Turkey where there is evidence that dancers wore leopard skins. Much more recently, in the 1800s and 1900s, many wealthy people wanted to hunt big game for the thrill of the chase. Big cat skins were used to decorate the hunters' houses, and their heads hung as trophies on the walls. Today, no one is allowed to hunt the endangered big cats anymore.

▲ **LION HUNT**
Egyptian rulers hunted lions from horse-drawn chariots. Hieroglyphics (picture writing) tell us of Pharaoh Amenophis III (1405–1367BC) who killed over 100 lions in the ten years of his rule. Some experts now think that the Egyptians may have bred lions specially to hunt them.

TIGER-HUNTING PRINCE ▶
This old painting on cotton shows an Indian prince hunting a tiger from the back of his elephant. Tiger hunting was a very popular pastime for many centuries in India until it was declared illegal in the 1970s.

▼ GREAT WHITE HUNTER

A hunting party proudly displays their tiger trophy. This photograph was taken in the 1860s. When India was under British rule, tiger hunting was considered to be a great sport by the British. Uncontrolled, ruthless hunting was a major cause of the tiger's dramatic fall in numbers.

▲ RITUAL ROBES

The Zulu chief Mangosothu Buthelezi wears wild cat skins on special occasions, like many African leaders and tribal healers. They are a sign of his rank and high status.

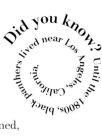

Did you know? Until the 1800s, black panthers lived near Los Angeles, California.

◄ CAT'S SKIN

A leopard is skinned, having been shot in the Okavango Delta, Botswana. Some game reserves raise money for conservation by charging huge sums to hunt. This only happens when numbers of a certain species are too large for the reserve.

SECOND SKIN ►

Some people continue to think it looks good to wear a coat made from the pelts of a wild cat. Many more, however, think that the fur looks much better on the cat. Designers now use fake fur and skins dyed to look like pelts, instead.

Big Cat Relatives

Fossil remains show that the ancestors of today's cats first roamed the Earth 65 million years ago. They were small animals called miacids. Scientists think that the miacids may be the forerunners of all carnivorous mammals on Earth today. About 35 million years ago the first cat-like carnivores appeared. Many of these early cats were large and dangerous creatures that have now become extinct (died out). The best-known are the sabre-toothed cats, which, unlike modern cats, used their canines for stabbing rather than biting. Fossil records of cats similar to modern cats date back about 10 million years. Today, there are 37 species of wild cat, big and small, and over 300 breeds of domestic cat.

▲ ANCIENT ANCESTOR

Miacids are thought to have been the first true carnivorous mammals. They first lived about 65 million years ago, around the same time that the dinosaurs died out. They are the first animals to have carnassial teeth – the strong back teeth used for shearing meat.

Did you know? The bones of sabre-tooth cats were found under Trafalgar Square, London.

◄ SABRE-TOOTH

This skeleton of a sabre-toothed cat called Smilodon is 15,000 years old. It was about the size of a present-day lion and lived in North America. Smilodon was a ferocious predator and hacked down mammoth and bison with its huge teeth.

124

◄ DOMESTIC CATS

Small cats are grouped under the genus *Felis*. Domestic or pet cats (*Felis catus*) are like miniature tamed versions of their wild relatives the big cats. They hunt, groom and leave scent marks just like wild cats. When a house cat rubs itself against a human, it is showing affection, but also putting its smell on that person.

Classification Chart

Kingdom	**Animalia** (all animals)	
Phylum	**Chordata** (animals with backbones)	
Class	**Mammalia** (animals with hair on their bodies that feed their young with milk)	
Order	**Carnivora** (mammals that eat meat)	
Family	**Felidae** (all cats)	
Genus	***Panthera*** (big cats)	
Species	***leo*** (lion)	

▲ CAT NAMES

Scientists classify (group) every cat within the animal kingdom and give it a Latin name. This chart shows how the lion is classified.

SERVAL ►

The serval (*Felis serval*) is a spotted, fleet-footed wild cat. It lives near water in southern and central Africa. Although it has long legs like a cheetah, it belongs to a different group and purrs like a domestic cat.

CARACAL ►

The caracal's (*Felis caracal*) most startling feature is the long tufts on its ears. These may help it locate prey. The caracal is related to both the leopard and the lynx. It lives in grasslands, open woodland and scrub in Africa and parts of Asia.

BOBCAT ►

The bobcat (*Felis rufus*) is related to the lynx (*Felis lynx*). Both have short tails and live in many sorts of habitats, but prefer the rocks and shrubby plants of mountain slopes. The bobcat is only found in northern North America where it is able to survive the harsh winter conditions.

Protecting Cats

All big cats are in danger of extinction. They are not only hunted for their skins, but for their teeth, bones and other body parts, which are used as traditional medicines in many countries. The Convention for International Trade in Endangered Species (CITES) lists all big cats under Appendix 1, which strictly controls their import and export. For cats particularly at risk, such as the tiger, all trade is banned. There are now many protected areas throughout the world where big cats can live without human interference. These areas are often not big enough, however, so the cats leave in search of food. They attack livestock and sometimes the local farmers.

▲ **IN ANCIENT TIMES**
A Roman mosaic showing a horseman hunting a leopard. Two thousand years ago, big cats were much more widespread. Until the 1900s, cheetahs lived throughout Africa, central India and the Middle East. Hunting big cats was not a problem when there were many big cats and not so many people, but now the situation is desperate.

▲ **GIR NATIONAL PARK**
The last remaining Asian lions live in the Gir National Park in western India. There are less than 300 lions living in the park. The Asian lion is slightly different to the African lion. It has a smaller mane and a fold of skin running between its front and back legs.

▲ **SERENGETI LION PROJECT**
This lion has been drugged so that it can be fitted with a radio collar, checked and then released. In the Serengeti National Park in Tanzania, scientists use methods like this to study lion behaviour.

▲ TIGER DETERRENT

Villagers in the Sundarbans mangrove forests in India wear masks on the backs of their heads. Tigers attack from behind, but will not usually strike if they see a face. The largest remaining tiger population in India is in the Sundarbans. Here 50 to 60 people die each year from attacks by tigers. There is obviously not enough food for the tigers, so conservationists are trying to improve the situation. Another deterrent is to set up dummies that look and smell like humans, but give out an electric shock if attacked. There are also electrified fences in some areas, and pigs are bred and released as tiger food.

▼ RADIO TRACKING

Biologists attach a radio collar to a tigress in the Chitwan National Park, Nepal. To save wild cats we need to understand their habits and their needs. For this reason, many scientists and conservationists are studying them. It is a very difficult task since cats are secretive and often nocturnal animals. One way of gathering information is to put a radio collar on a big cat and then follow its movements. By doing this, the animal can be tracked at long range.

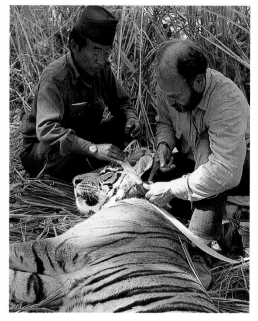

The Great Sphinx

In Egypt, an enormous statue with a human head and the body of a lion guards the Great Pyramids at Giza. This statue is the Great Sphinx. A story written in 1419BC on the Sphinx tells of a prince called Thutmose IV who fell asleep between the paws of the statue. He dreamt that the Sun god told him to take away the sand covering part of the Sphinx and he would become a king. When he awoke, Thutmose did as he had been instructed, and the dream came true.

Bears and Pandas

Michael Bright

Consultant: Dr Douglas Richardson,
Zoological Director, Rome Zoo

The Bear Facts

Bears may look large, cuddly and appealing, but in reality they are enormously powerful animals. Bears are mammals with bodies covered in thick fur. They are heavily built with short tails and large claws. All bears are carnivores (meat-eaters), but most enjoy a very mixed diet with the occasional snack of meat. The exception is the polar bear, which feasts on the blubber (fat) of seals. There are eight living species of bear: the brown bear, American black bear, Asiatic black bear, polar bear, sun bear, sloth bear, spectacled bear and the giant panda. They live in both cold and tropical regions of the world. Bears are loners and their nature is unpredictable, which makes them potentially dangerous to people.

WINNIE-THE-POOH
The lovable teddy bear Winnie-the-Pooh was created by A.A. Milne. Like real bears he loved honey. Teddy bears became popular as toys in the early 1900s. The President of the U.S.A. Theodore Roosevelt refused to shoot a bear cub on a hunting trip. Toy bears went on sale soon after known as "teddy's bears".

◀ BEAR FACE
The brown bear shares the huge dog-like head and face of all bears. Bears have prominent noses, but relatively small eyes and ears. This is because they mostly rely on their sense of smell to help them find food.

▲ BIG FLAT FEET
A polar bear's feet are broad, flat and furry. The five long, curved claws cannot be retracted (pulled back). One swipe could kill a seal instantly.

Thick fur covers a
heavily-built body.

POINTS OF A BEAR

The brown bear is called the grizzly
bear in North America. Fully-grown
brown bears weigh nearly half a tonne.
They fear no other animals apart from
humans. They can chase prey at high
speed, but they rarely bother as
they feed mainly on plants.

A bear has a large head,
with small eyes and
erect, rounded ears.

The long, prominent,
dog-like snout
dominates the face.

▲ GIANT PANDA

China's giant panda, with its distinctive
black and white coat, is a very unusual
bear. Unlike most other bears, which
will eat anything, pandas feed almost
exclusively on the bamboo plant.

A bear's main
strength is in its
massive shoulders
and front legs.

Its broad, flat feet
have long claws.

◀ ARCTIC NOMAD

Most bears lead a solitary life. The polar bear
wanders alone across the Arctic sea ice.
Usually it will not tolerate other
bears. The exceptions are
bears that congregate at
rubbish dumps, or
mothers accompanied
by their cubs as
shown here.

131

Sloth bear
(Melursus ursinus)

▲ **SLOTH BEAR**

Long curved claws, a mobile snout and long fur are the distinguishing features of the sloth bear. It lives in India and Sri Lanka and feeds mainly on insects called termites and fruit.

Size of a Bear

The two largest bears in the world are the powerful polar bear and the brown bears of Kodiak Island, Alaska. Kodiak bears grow up to 2.8m long and weigh, on average, up to 443kg, while polar bears have a maximum length of 3m and weigh as much as 650kg. Brown bears in Europe and Asia are generally smaller than grizzlies (American brown bears). The largest is the Kamchatka brown bear of eastern Russia. A full size adult grizzly weighs as much as a bison and even the smallest is bigger than a wolf. The smallest bear is the sun bear at 1.4m long and weighing 65kg. In between are American and Asiatic black bears (both 1.7m long and up to 120kg), the spectacled bear (2.1m long, up to 200kg) and the sloth bear (1.9m long, up to 115kg).

American black bear
(Ursus americanus)

▼ **SPECTACLED BEAR**

The South American spectacled bear gets its name from the distinctive markings on its face. It is the only bear found in South America and is a good climber.

Spectacled bear
(Tremarctos ornatus)

▲ **AMERICAN BLACK BEAR**

There are ten times as many black bears as brown bears living in the forests of North America. Black bears resemble small brown bears except that they lack a shoulder hump.

Polar bear
(Ursus maritimus)

◀ **ICE GIANT**

The male polar bear is a giant among
bears. It is bigger than most brown bears,
but less robustly built, with a longer
head and neck. Female polar bears are
much smaller, weighing less than half
a fully-grown adult male. Polar bears
live in the frozen wastes of the Arctic.
They can swim in the icy sea, protected
by insulating fur and layers of thick fat.

Brown bear
(Ursus arctos)

▶ **BIG BROWN BEARS**

The brown bear is the most widely found bear,
living in Europe, Asia and North America. Its size
varies in different parts of the world. This is due
to diet and climate rather than any genetic
differences. For example, large Kodiak bears
catch a lot of protein-rich salmon.

Did you know? Kodiak brown bears weigh up to 750kg. The heaviest known

▼ **THE SUN BEAR**

The sun bear is the smallest of all the bears.
It lives in the thick forests of South-east
Asia. Because it lives in a hot tropical
climate, the sun bear also has
a short coat. Its feet have naked soles
and long, curved claws, which can grip
well when climbing trees.

Sun bear
(Helarctos malayanus)

133

Giant panda
(Ailuropoda melanoleuca)

Giant Pandas

Scientists have argued for many years about whether or not the giant panda is a bear. In 1869, the first Western naturalist to see a giant panda identified it as a bear. But a year later, scientists examined a panda skeleton and decided it was more like a raccoon. This was because the giant panda's skeleton shared some features with the red panda, an earlier discovery that had been grouped with the raccoon family. The giant panda certainly looks like a bear, but it does not behave like one. It does not hibernate, although it lives in places with very cold winters. It rarely roars like a bear, but tends to bleat. Recent genetic studies and comparisons with other animals, however, indicate that the panda's nearest relatives are bears and that the giant panda is indeed a bear.

▲ UP A TREE

Giant pandas sometimes climb trees to avoid enemies. They also scrape trees with their claws. This is a sign that says KEEP OUT to other pandas. Pandas are about 1.7m long and weigh up to 125kg. They are the only surviving members of the earliest group of bears to evolve. Fossils of giant pandas have only ever been discovered in Thailand and China.

▶ RED PANDA

The red panda is a member of the raccoon family and lives in the high bamboo forests of southern Asia. It has several similarities to the giant panda, including skull shape, tooth structure and a false thumb to hold bamboo.

Red panda
(Ailurus fulgens)

134

▶ BAMBOO BEAR

The giant panda of western China spends 10 to 12 hours a day eating bamboo. Its massive head contains large chewing muscles needed to break up the tough bamboo. It has a simple stomach and short gut, however, which are features of a meat-eating carnivore and make digesting bamboo hard work. The giant panda's large shoulders and reduced hindquarters give it a curious, shambling walk.

Giant panda
(Ailuropoda melanoleuca)

Raccoon *(Procyon lotor)*

▲ FALSE THUMB

The giant panda has a false thumb on its forepaw. This is a modified wrist bone used to hold narrow bamboo shoots. A giant panda's massive skull is quite distinct from the smaller, more slender skull of the raccoon. The raccoon (*Procyon lotor*) does not have a false thumb, unlike its relative the red panda.

▼ AMERICAN BANDIT

The inquisitive raccoon is a close relative of bears. It lives in North America and uses its front paws to capture small aquatic prey, such as freshwater crayfish. It also scavenges through the remains of human waste.

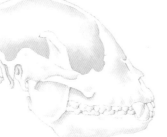

Raccoon
(Procyon lotor)

135

Bones and Teeth

Bears have a large and massive skull, a solidly
built skeleton, relatively short and stocky
limbs, a small tail and short feet. Each foot
has five equal-sized digits (toes), with strong,
curved claws for digging and tearing.
The claws cannot be retracted (pulled back)
so are constantly worn down. In most bears'
jaws, the carnassial teeth (large meat-
shearing teeth) common to all carnivores are
reduced or even missing. Instead, bears have
broad flat molars for crushing plant food.
Only the polar bear has flesh-slicing
carnassials to deal with its animal prey.
The sloth bear is also unusual because it lacks
the inner pair of upper incisors (front teeth).
This helps it suck up insects from their nests.

▲ A MIGHTY ROAR
As this bear roars, it bares its large
canine teeth. However, on average
only 20 per cent of a brown bear's
diet is made up of animal flesh.
Instead, bears rely on their large
molars to crush their vegetable food.

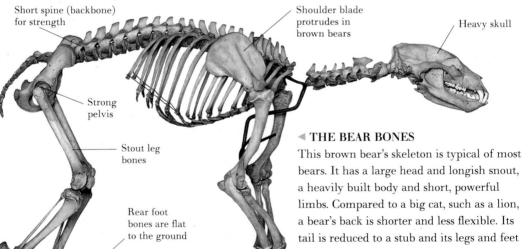

Short spine (backbone) for strength

Shoulder blade protrudes in brown bears

Heavy skull

Strong pelvis

Stout leg bones

Rear foot bones are flat to the ground

Front feet are slightly raised

◄ THE BEAR BONES
This brown bear's skeleton is typical of most
bears. It has a large head and longish snout,
a heavily built body and short, powerful
limbs. Compared to a big cat, such as a lion,
a bear's back is shorter and less flexible. Its
tail is reduced to a stub and its legs and feet
are shorter and heavier. The shoulder
hump seen in brown bears is due
to their protruding shoulder bones.

Canine tooth

Carnassial tooth

▲ SHORT FACE

This brown bear's skull is shorter and more robust than that of the polar bear. North American brown bears tend to have larger skulls than bears in other parts of the world.

▲ LONG FACE

This polar bear's skull is longer and more slender than that of other bears. Like other carnivores, it has prominent, dagger-like canine teeth and meat-slicing carnassials at the back.

▲ PRIMITIVE BEAR

The spectacled bear is grouped separately from other bears. Apart from the giant panda, it is the most primitive bear. Its short muzzle and the unique arrangement of teeth in its jaw give it a more rounded head shape than its fellow bears.

▲ GIANT PANDA

The giant panda has the most massive skull in relation to its size of all living bears. Its round face and head are the result of large jaw muscles needed to grind tough bamboo stems.

▶ SLENDER SWIMMING BEAR

The polar bear has a more elongated body than other bears. Its neck and skull are relatively long and slim. These are adaptations that help the bear to swim through the water by streamlining its body. It also has lower shoulders, well-developed hindquarters and large, broad feet.

137

Strong Muscles

Bears are the bully-boys of the animal kingdom. Their strength is mainly in the muscles of their legs and shoulders. Unlike cats and dogs, which run on their toes for speed, bears walk on the flat soles of their broad feet, just as humans do. What bears lack in speed they make up for in strength. Their powerful, mobile limbs can be put to good use digging, climbing, fishing and fighting. They will attack others of their own kind and defend themselves ably from enemies. In a fight, a bear can do considerable damage and survives by sheer brute force. Male bears are generally much larger than females of the same species.

▲ **CLAWS DOWN**
The sun bear has particularly large, curved claws for climbing trees. It spends most of the day sleeping or sunbathing in the branches. At night it strips off bark with its claws, looking for insects and honey in bees' nests.

◀ **PUTTING ON WEIGHT**
This grizzly bear is at peak size. Most bears change size as the seasons pass. They are large and well-fed in autumn, ready for their winter hibernation. When they emerge in spring, they are scrawny with sagging coats.

BEOWULF
An Anglo-Saxon poem tells of the hero Beowulf (bear-wolf). He had the strength of a bear and went through many heroic adventures. Beowulf is famous for slaying a monster called Grendel. Here, Beowulf as an old man lies dying from the wounds inflicted by a fire-breathing dragon.

Lungs   Diaphragm   Liver   Kidney   Relatively short intestines are typical of a meat-eater

Trachea (windpipe)

Heart

The stomach has a single chamber, not many chambers like other plant-eaters

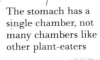

▲ INSIDE A BEAR

Although bears mainly eat plants, they have the relatively short intestines more characteristic of a meat-eater, rather than a long gut like a cow. This makes it hard for them to digest their food. Curiously, the bamboo-eating giant panda has the shortest gut of all. Because of this it can digest no more than 20 per cent of what it eats, compared to 60 per cent in a cow.

Bears are plantigrade, which means they walk on the soles of their feet

▲ SHORT BURSTS

Bears are not particularly agile and swift, but they can run fast over short distances. The brown bear can charge at 50km/h (lions reach about 65km/h) and does sometimes chase its food. A bear at full charge is a frightening sight and quickly scares away enemies.

▲ SWEET TOOTH

The sun bear's long slender tongue is ideal for licking honey from bees' nests and for scooping up termites and other insects. Like all bears it has mobile lips, a flexible snout and strong jaws.

139

Warm Fur

All bears have thick fur all over their bodies, including the face. Ground-living bears even have fur between the pads of their feet, while the soles of tree-climbing bears are naked. A thick coat insulates well in the cold, but can cause overheating in summer, so many bears moult. Most bears' coats tend to be brown, black, cinnamon (reddish-brown), grey or white and some have face and chest markings. The most strikingly marked bear is the giant panda. Its startling black and white pattern blends in with the shadowy bamboo of its mountain home. This is particularly so at dawn and dusk, the panda's most active times. In winter, against snow, black rocks and trees, the panda is almost invisible.

▲ **WHITE BEAR**
The Chinese call the giant panda *bei-shung* (white bear). It is considered to be basically white with black ears, eye patches, legs and shoulders. Sometimes the black areas have a chestnut reddish tinge.

▲ **VELVET COAT**
The sun bear has relatively short fur, a bit like velvet. It is generally black with a grey to orange muzzle and pale feet. Some bears have white or pale orange-yellow, crescent-shaped markings on the chest.

BERSERKIR
Among the most feared of Viking warriors were berserkirs. They were named after the bear pelts or bear-skin shirts they wore. Berserkirs worked themselves up into a frenzy before battle. We still use the Norse word berserk to mean crazy or wild. This walrus ivory berserkir is part of a chess set from the island of Lewis off the west coast of Scotland. The berserkir is shown biting his shield and clasping his sword in the rage of battle.

▲ **BEAR FOOT**

The broad, flat paw of a brown bear has thick fur on the upper surface and some between the toes, too. Ground-living bears, such as the brown bear, use their claws to hold on to a salmon or to catch and kill a young deer.

▼ **SILVER TIP**

The grizzly (American brown bear) gets its name from the way in which the long hairs of the shoulders and back are frosted with white. This gives the bear's coat a grizzled appearance. Brown bears, like the grizzly, are usually a dark brown colour, but they may also be any shade between light cream and black.

▲ **FACIAL MARKINGS**

The spectacled bear is generally dark brown or black. It has an unmistakable, spectacle-like pattern of white or yellowish hairs around the eyes and across the nose. These markings may extend to the chest.

▶ **LONG HAIR**

The sloth bear has long, black shaggy fur. The longest hair is between the shoulders. The black fur can be tinged with brown or grey. There is a white, or yellow to chestnut-brown, patch in the shape of a U or Y on the bear's chest. Chest markings may act as a warning sign when the bear stands up.

141

Life on the Ice

The polar bear is perfectly adapted to life in the frozen Arctic, where winter temperatures can drop to -50°C. Beneath its skin lies a thick layer of fat. The bear's entire body, including the soles of the feet, is covered in insulating fur made up of thick hairs with a woolly underfur. Each hair is not actually white, but translucent and hollow. This acts like a tiny greenhouse, allowing light and heat from the sun to pass through, trapping the warm air. Sometimes, such as in zoos, the hairs are invaded by tiny algae and the polar bear's coat has a green tinge. In the wild, the fur often appears yellow, the result of oil stains from its seal prey. Beneath the fur the skin is black, which absorbs heat. This excellent insulation keeps the polar bear's body at a constant 37°C.

RESPECT FOR THE ICE BEAR

The polar bear is the most powerful spirit in Arctic cultures. The Inuit believe that a polar bear has a soul. It will only allow itself to be killed if the hunter treats it properly after death. It is forbidden to hunt another bear too soon. Time must be left for the bear's soul to return to its family. Some Inuit offer a dead male bear a miniature bow and arrow, and a female bear a needle holder.

◄ **SEA-GOING BEAR**
Polar bears are excellent swimmers. They must swim frequently for their icy world is unpredictable. In winter, the Arctic Ocean freezes over. But with the arrival of storms and warmer weather the ice breaks up. Then the bear must swim between ice floes in search of seals. The thick layer of fat below the skin and dense, insulating fur allow a polar bear to swim in the coldest seas without suffering. In such cold water, a human being would be dead in a few minutes.

▲ COOLING DOWN

Polar bears are so well insulated they are in danger of overheating on warm days. To keep cool, they lie flat out on the ice. At other times they lie on their backs with their feet in the air.

▲ BEAR SLUMBERS

A polar bear, like a human, sleeps for seven or eight hours at a time. This helps the polar bear to conserve energy and heat. Polar bears are not at risk of attack when they are sleeping, so they do not have to hide like other animals. Most often, polar bears find a sheltered area to protect them from the cold polar winds.

▲ WARM BEARS

The insulating fur and fat of a polar bear is so efficient that little heat is lost. In fact, if a scientist were to look at a polar bear with an infra-red camera (which detects heat given off by the body), only the bear's nose and eyes would be visible.

▲ LAZY DAYS

Polar bears are most active at the start of the day. During summer, when the ice melts and retreats, bears may be prevented from hunting seals. Then they rest, living off their fat reserves and eating berries.

Using Brain and Senses

All bears are very intelligent. Size for size, they have larger brains than other carnivores, such as dogs and cats. They can remember sources of food and are very curious. Bears use their brains to find food or a mate, and to stay out of trouble. They are mainly solitary plant-eaters, however, so they have little need to think up hunting tactics or ways of communication. They rely on smell (the part of their brains that detects scent is the largest of any carnivore), with small eyes and ears compared to their head size. Bears often appear short-sighted, although they have colour vision to recognize edible fruits and nuts. People can easily chance upon a bear and take it by surprise, prompting the startled animal to attack in self-defence.

▼ SCENT MARKING
An American black bear cub practises marking a tree by scratching. When it is older, the bear will leave a scent mark to indicate to other bears that the territory is occupied.

◀ TEMPER TANTRUM
A threatened bear puts on a fierce display. First it beats the ground or vegetation with its front feet. Then it stands up on its back legs to look larger. This is accompanied by a high-pitched snorting through open lips or a series of hoarse barks. The display of aggression finishes with snapping the jaws together.

▲ FOLLOW YOUR NOSE

A brown bear relies more on smell than sight. It often raises its head and sniffs the air to check out who or what is about. It can detect the faintest trace of a smell, searching for others of its kind.

▼ GETTING TO KNOW YOU

Polar bear cubs rub against their mother to spread her scent over themselves. Smell allows a mother and cubs to recognize each other. They also communicate with sounds. Distressed cubs make low-pitched snores that develop into high whines.

BRUNO THE BEAR

Aesop's Fables are a set of tales written by the ancient Greek writer Aesop. One fable features Bruno the bear. He is shown as stupid and easily deceived. Bears were considered slow-witted because they sleep a lot. But Bruno was kind, unlike the cunning Reynard the fox. Bruno cared about others and forgave those who played pranks on him. Bruno was the forerunner of characters such as Winnie-the-Pooh.

▲ SNOWY SCENT TRAIL

Even in the Arctic, polar bears can pick up the trails of other bears and follow them. There are few objects around to use as scent posts for polar bears, so trails may be marked by the dribbling of urine on the ground.

Finding Food

Most bears eat whatever is available at
different times of the year. They have binges
and put on fat in times of plenty, then fast
when food is scarce. Brown bears are typical
of most bears in that they eat an enormous
variety of food, from grasses, herbs and
berries to ants and other insects. They also
catch salmon and rodents, and on rare
occasions hunt down bigger game, such as
caribou, seals and birds. Only polar bears eat
almost entirely meat, especially young seals.
In summer, however, as the ice melts and
they are unable to hunt, polars supplement
their diet with grasses and berries. All bears,
even the bamboo-loving panda, also
scavenge on the carcasses of prey left by
other animals. They are attracted to
easy food, and rummage through
rubbish thrown out into dustbins
and left behind in campsites.

GOLDILOCKS
The famous story of Goldilocks and
the Three Bears *was first told in
1837. In the story, the bears and
their ability to organize themselves
properly are used to make a strong
moral point. In contrast, Goldilocks
is shown as a foolish, unthinking
girl, who gets a nasty fright.*

> ### HUNTING DOWN A MEAL

This American black bear has caught a white-tailed
deer fawn. Both black and brown bears are successful
hunters. They are able to ambush large animals and kill
them by using their considerable bulk, strong paws
and jaws. The size of the bear determines the size of
its prey. Large brown bears may prey on moose,
caribou, bison, musk ox, seals and stranded whales.
Black bears are smaller than brown bears and take
smaller prey, such as deer fawns, lemmings and
hares. Roots, fruit, seeds and nuts, however, form
up to 80 per cent of brown and black bears' diets.

▶ WALRUS CITY

Polar bears arrive on the northern coast of Russia each year to hunt walruses that have come there to breed. Enormous adult walruses shrug off attacks, but the young walrus pups are more vulnerable.

▲ BEACHCOMBING

Brown bears are attracted to beaches beside rivers and in estuaries. They overturn stones to feed on aquatic creatures, such as crabs and crayfish, that are hiding underneath.

▲ FRUIT LOVERS

An American black bear snacks on the ripe berries of a mountain ash tree. It carefully uses its incisors (front teeth) to strip the berries from their woody stem.

▲ INSECT EATERS

Two sloth bear cubs learn to dig up termites. The sloth bear uses its sickle-shaped claws to break open ant hills, bees' nests and termite mounds. Because it feeds mainly on termites, it has an ingenious way of collecting its insect food. First it blows away the dust. Then it forms a suction tube with its mouth and tongue, through which it can vacuum up its food.

Focus on

The giant panda specializes in eating bamboo, which forms over 99 per cent of its diet. Bamboo is plentiful and easy to harvest. Pandas consume the sprouts, stems and leaves. Digesting bamboo, however, is hard work. This is because the giant panda has a simple stomach and a short gut more characteristic of a carnivore. Most herbivores, such as cows, have several stomachs and very long intestines with bacteria inside that break down the plant tissue. The panda does not, so it must feed on huge quantities of bamboo (up to 40 kg) every day in order to keep going. Much of the leaf and stem matter passes through undigested.

MEAT AND TWO VEG

Whilst pandas spend most of their time eating bamboo, they do sometimes supplement their diet with meat when they can get it. They catch rats and beetles in the bamboo stands, and have been known to scavenge at leopard kills. But they make clumsy hunters and easy prey is scarce. In contrast bamboo is very abundant.

EARLY RISER

The giant panda is most active in the early morning and late afternoon. It spends 16 or more hours a day feeding and sleeps for up to four hours at a time. Most of the water a panda needs comes from bamboo. If it is thirsty, it scoops out a hollow by a stream. When this is full, the panda drinks all it can.

Bamboo Bears

ESSENTIAL FOOD

Umbrella bamboo and arrow bamboo are the giant panda's favourite food. Pandas also eat 28 other species of bamboo. They favour the leaves over the stems because these are the most nutritious parts and are easiest to digest. Pandas also eat other plants such as juniper, vines, holly and wild parsnip.

FEEDING ALL YEAR

Since bamboo is green and nutritious throughout the year, even in winter, the panda has a continuous supply of food. Unlike other bears, whose food is scarce at certain times, the panda has no need to hibernate, even when snow is covering its mountain home. A thick fur coat protects it from the cold.

TABLE MANNERS

A panda usually feeds sitting upright on its haunches. This leaves its forelegs free to handle bamboo. It manipulates the long stems of bamboo using its extra thumb (actually a modified wrist bone) on its front paws. It strips away the woody outer covering with its teeth. Then it pushes the stem at right angles into the corner of its mouth. Here, the centre part is crushed by large back teeth and then swallowed.

Climbing Trees

Trees provide food for some bears and a place of safety for others. Sun bears, sloth bears and spectacled bears climb trees regularly in search of food, such as fruits, seeds and nuts, as well as birds' eggs. Black bears are also agile tree-climbers. Polar bears rarely encounter trees. Those that move into the forest during the summer months, however, rest in hollows dug among tree roots to avoid the heat. Brown bear cubs climb trees to escape danger, but adult brown bears are too heavy to be good climbers. A female sloth bear will carry her small cubs into a tree on her back, unless she is escaping from a leopard since they can also climb trees! Most bears also use trees to mark their territory. They scratch the bark and rub on scents to tell other bears they are there.

◀ TREE-TOP HOME

The sun bear seeks out termite and bees' nests, and will rip away bark to get at insects hidden underneath. Although the sun bear feeds mainly on insects it also eats ripe fruit and preys on small rodents, birds and lizards.

▶ BEAR DANGER

A mother American black bear sends her cubs up into a tree while she stands guard at its base. If the danger is from an adult brown bear, the female will flee and return later for her cubs when the grizzly has gone.

▲ BELOW THE BARK

An adult, cinnamon-coloured American black bear is able to climb into a tree with ease using its short but sturdy claws. It can also lift bark to lick out insects with a long tongue.

▲ UP A TREE

Giant pandas stay mainly on the ground, but they will climb trees occasionally. They do so to sun themselves or to rest. Female pandas sometimes head up a tree to escape males, while males climb trees to advertise their presence.

▼ SAFE HAVEN

Black bears are normally found in forested areas. They have favourite trees located along trails where bears and other animals regularly pass. The bear marks the tree base with its scent and climbs into the branches where it is safe from brown bears.

Short, sturdy claws on a black bear's feet make tree climbing easy

▲ HIGH SCHOOL

Black bear cubs stay close to their mother both on the ground and in a tree. They watch and learn from her how to climb and find food among the branches.

▼ TREE HOUSE

Spectacled bears pull branches together to make a feeding platform. From here the bears feed mainly on tough plants called bromeliads. They also eat fruits, nuts, and honey and may take mice, rabbits and insects.

Gone Fishing

Brown and black bears sometimes overcome their reluctance to be with other bears when there is plenty of food available. This happens regularly on the rivers of the northwest coast of North America. Here, thousands of salmon come in from the sea and head upriver to spawn. The bears fish alongside each other at sites such as rapids where the water is shallower and the salmon are swimming more slowly. An uneasy truce exists between the bears, although isolated fights do occur. The salmon runs take place at different times of the year, but the most important are those in the months leading up to winter. The bears catch the oil-rich salmon to obtain the extra fat they need for the long hibernation ahead.

▲ STRIPPED TO THE BONE
Having caught a fish, the bear holds it firmly in its forepaws. Then it strips away the skin and flesh from the bones.

◀ SALMON LEAP
Salmon sometimes jump right into a bear's mouth. The bear stands at the edge of a small waterfall. Here the salmon must leap clear of the water to continue their journey upriver. All the bear needs to do is open its mouth!

◄ COME INTO CONFLICT

Sometimes the uncertain truce between bears breaks down and they fight for the best fishing sites in the river. Young bears playfight, but older ones fight for real. An open mouth, showing the long canine teeth, is a warning to an opponent. If the intruder fails to back down it is attacked. Fights are often soon over, because the bears are quick to return to the abundant source of fish.

▲ FISHING LESSON

Bear cubs watch closely as their mother catches a salmon. The cubs learn by example and will eventually try it themselves. It will be a long time before they are as skilful as their mother.

▲ A SLOUTHE OF BEERYS

A group of bears is called a sloth, so brown bears on a salmon river are a sloth of grizzlies. The term "a slouthe of beerys" was used in the Middle Ages. It came from people's belief at the time that bears were slow and lazy.

153

Focus on

Because it lives in one of the harshest and most unpredictable places on Earth, the polar bear is constantly on the look out for food. There may be four or five days between meals. Their most common prey is the ringed seal, although harp, bearded and hooded seals, or young walruses, are also taken. In spring, a bear searches for seal nursery dens. It breaks through the roof of snow and ice to reach the seal pups inside by jumping down with its powerful forelegs. During the rest of the year, a bear searches for holes in the ice where seals come up to breathe. While its eyesight and hearing are similar to ours, a polar bear's sense of smell is far superior. It can smell a den or breathing hole from a kilometre away.

1 A polar bear uses stealth and surprise to catch its prey. The bear approaches its target slowly, moving silently across the ice and swimming between ice floes. Its broad paws act like paddles and propel it effectively through the water. Its hind legs trail in the water and steer like a ship's rudder. A polar bear can also swim underwater to reach its prey, erupting from the sea to surprise seals resting on the edge of the ice.

2 A polar bear will stand or lie motionless for hours beside a good place for hunting. This may be at a seal's breathing hole or den. In spring, cracks form in the ice where it begins to melt. At points along the ice, seals emerge to rest or bask in the sun. A bear sniffs out suitable hauling-out places and lies in wait. Often, the bear's patience is not rewarded, for only one in fifty attempts to catch prey are successful.

Seal Hunting

3 A harp seal pops up to breathe through a hole in the ice. Before surfacing it would have looked for signs of danger. A bear usually lies on its stomach with its chin close to the edge of the ice. This conceals it from sight until the seal surfaces.

4 When a seal surfaces the bear scoops it out with a paw or grasps it around the head with its teeth and flips it out on to the ice. A powerful bite to the head crushes the seal's skull or breaks its neck and kills it instantly. The bear eats the fat and internal organs, but not the meat unless it is very hungry. It eats quickly since the smell of the kill might attract other bears.

5 Arctic foxes often follow polar bears across the ice in order to take advantage of their leftovers. Polar bears feed mainly on the seal blubber (fat), leaving behind most of the meat and bones. An average bear needs to eat 2kg of seal fat a day to survive. They have huge stomachs, enabling them to eat much more. After the meal, a polar bear cleans its fur by swirling in the water or rolling in the snow.

Winter Shutdown

Black bears, brown bears and pregnant female polar bears hibernate. They do so because food is scarce, not because of the cold. Scientists argued for years whether bears truly hibernate or merely doze during the winter months. Now, according to recent research, the hibernation of bears is thought to be even more complete than that of small mammals. During hibernation, a brown bear's heart rate drops to about 35 beats per minute, half its normal rate. American black bears reduce their blood temperature by at least one degree. They do not eat or drink for up to four months. Bears survive only on the fat that they have stored during the summer. A bear might have lost up to 50 per cent of its body-weight by the end of the winter.

▲ **FAT BEARS**
Before the winter hibernation a bear can become quite obese. Fat reserves make up over half this black bear's body-weight. It needs this bulk to make sure that it has sufficient fat on its body to survive the winter fast. In the weeks leading up to hibernation, a bear must consume large quantities of energy-rich foods, such as salmon.

Did you know? Some hibernating bears sleep for 5½ months non-stop.

◀ **HOME COMFORTS**
A brown bear pulls in grass and leaves to cushion its winter den. American black bears and brown bears sleep in small, specially dug dens. These are usually found on the sunny, south-facing slopes of mountains.

▲ SCANDINAVIAN REFUGE

A hole dug by a brown bear serves as its winter den in this Swedish forest. Bears spend winter in much stranger places, such as under cabins occupied by people, under bridges or beside busy roads.

▲ READY FOR ACTION

If disturbed, a bear wakes easily from its winter sleep. Although it is dormant, a bear's body is ready for action. It is able to defend itself immediately against predators, such as a hungry wolf pack.

▲ SNOW HOUSE

Female polar bears leave the drifting floes in winter and head inland to excavate a nursery den. They dig deep down into the snow and ice, tunnelling about 5m into the ground. Here they will give birth to their cubs. In severe weather, a male polar bear rests by lying down and allowing itself to be covered by an insulating layer of snow.

▲ WINTER NURSERY

In the early winter, one bear enters a den, but three might emerge in spring. Female polar bears, like most bears, give birth (usually to twins) while hidden away in their dens. The tiny cubs are born in the middle of winter, in December or January.

A Solitary Life

Bears do not like other bears. They prefer to be alone. When two bears meet there is sometimes a fight, but usually it is just a shouting match and display. Young bears have playfights, not serious contests but rehearsals for battles later in life. Bears will break off hostilities when food is plentiful. Brown bears tolerate each other at fishing rivers and polar bears scavenge together at whale carcasses and rubbish dumps. But bears have to be constantly wary of other bears. Cannibalism (eating members of the same species) is more common in bears than in any other mammals. Male bears will fight and kill cubs. Deadly fights between adult male bears may end in one killing the other and then feeding on the loser's body.

▲ CANNIBALISM
Adult American male black bears and male polar bears are cannibals. They eat mainly younger bears. However, this sort of behaviour is thought to be relatively rare.

◄ ICE DANCE
Like two ballet dancers, young male polar bears play at fighting. They use exaggerated lunges and swipes with their paws and jaws. They do not hurt each other, but they must learn to fight well. Later in life as fully grown adults they will compete with other males for females during the breeding season. Fights between well-matched individuals can be violent and often bloody.

158

THE JUNGLE BOOK

Rudyard Kipling's famous story The Jungle Book *was first published in 1894. A young boy named Mowgli is brought up by wolves. He is befriended by Baloo the bear and Bagheera the panther who teach him the law of the jungle. The tiger Shere Khan plots to kill the man-cub.*

▲ TRAGEDY ON THE ICE

A mother polar bear stands over her cub, which has been mauled by a male. Male polar bears usually kill cubs for food. The female attacks and tries to drive the male away. Males are much bigger than females, but a female with cubs is a fierce opponent.

▲ FRIENDS AT THE FEAST

Brown bears gather to catch salmon at a popular spot in Alaska. If they get too close to each other, the bears will contest their fishing rights. Usually the larger bears succeed in fishing the best sites.

▲ FISHING BREAK

Young brown bears take a break from learning to fish and practise fighting instead. They fight by pushing and shoving at each other, using their enormous bulk to overcome their opponent. They also try to bite each other around the head and neck.

Meeting a Mate

Brown and black bears mate in the summer between May and July. Males use their well-developed sense of smell to track down females in heat. Brown bears often group together near rich food sources in the mating season, so males have to fight each other for the right to mate. Courtship between male and female bears is very brief, but when the male finds the female is ready to mate, he tries to isolate her from other males. The female is pregnant for from six to nine months. The length varies, because, no matter the time of mating, all the cubs are born at roughly the same time in the new year. This is because female bears delay the development of the fertilized egg in their wombs until late summer.

▲ COURTING COUPLE
A male and female brown bear may stay together for over a week during courtship and mate several times. The act of mating stimulates the female to release an egg. The male keeps other male bears away to be sure he is the father of any offspring.

◄ LOOK!
Male giant pandas often climb trees to advertise to females they are willing to mate. They wail, yap and bark to attract attention. Their loud calls also attract other males. The most dominant male mates with the female first. Pandas mate in spring.

▲ COURTSHIP DEADLOCK
A male has to overcome the female's natural tendency to be wary of him. The two assess each other with some gentle sparring interrupted by brief stand-offs and a lot of sniffing.

▼ HEAVENLY SCENT

Bears rely on their keen sense of smell to find a partner. An Alaskan brown bear approaches a receptive female, checking her odour track on the ground. If she lets him approach he sniffs her head, body and rear for signs that she is ready to mate. This period of courtship can last for up to 15 days, before the female is finally ready.

▶ ARCTIC ENGAGEMENT

Polar bears mate from late March to late May. They tend to congregate where there are plenty of seals. There are usually more males willing to mate than females. Like brown bears, a successful male tries to keep his temporary partner away from other male bears. They mate many times over a period of a week or more.

◀ MATING TIME

If a female brown bear is receptive, the male places his paw on her back. He mounts and grasps her in a bear hug, and bites the back of her head and neck. Mating is brief, lasting for only a few seconds up to about three minutes. The pair may mate up to 16 times in one day, and this may be repeated over several days. This ensures the female becomes pregnant by that particular male.

161

Nursery Dens

Most bears give birth hidden away from the outside world in dens. American black and brown bear cubs are born in winter, in January and February, when their mother is closeted in her winter den. A den can be a cave, in a hollow tree, under a tree that has been pushed over by the wind, or in a self-made hollow. Usually, two to three cubs are born, naked and helpless. Newborn bear cubs are small for the size of their mother. This is because a female bear's gestation period is very short. The mother has also to rely only on her fat reserves to build up their tiny bodies. A mother bear is only able to feed her cubs if she has eaten enough food in the months before her winter hibernation.

▲ **BLIND AND HELPLESS**
Ten-day-old brown bear cubs nestle into their mother's fur for warmth. With their eyes and ears tightly closed shut, they are totally dependent on her. The cubs remain in the den until May or June when they are about four months old.

Did you know? Polar bear cubs are no bigger than guinea pigs when born.

◀ **TWINS**
A polar bear mother tends her two young. The family leaves its den between late February and April depending on where they live. The further north they are, the later in the year they emerge.

▲ **TRIPLETS**

This American black bear has given birth to three healthy cubs. Females may have up to four cubs at one time. About the size of a rat and naked at first, the cubs grow quickly. They will leave the den in April or May.

▲ **PANDA BABY**

At Wolong breeding station in Sichuan, China, a baby giant panda is put in a box to be weighed. Giant pandas give birth to one or two cubs in a cave or tree hollow. If twins are born the mother often only rears one, leaving the other to die.

◄ **MOTHER'S MILK**

Three-month-old polar bear cubs suckle on their mother's milk. The milk is rich in fats and the cubs suckle for up to a year. Polar bear cubs are born covered with fine hair.

▶ **IN THE DEN**

American black bears weigh less than 300g when they are born in late January or early February. Their small size and lack of fur makes them vulnerable to the cold. The mother cleans and dries the cubs, then cuddles them close. The den is lined with branches, leaves, herbs and grasses to make a warm blanket. The mother spends a lot of time grooming her cubs and keeps the den scrupulously clean by eating their droppings.

Focus on

1 A bank of snow makes an ideal site for a polar bear's winter den. The pregnant female bear digs into the south side of the snowdrift. The prevailing northerly winds pile up snow on the other side.

From late October, a pregnant female polar bear digs a snow den. Usually it is on a slope facing south, some distance from the sea. This is where she will give birth to her cubs. The mother warms her den with heat from her body. A tunnel to the nursery chamber slopes upwards so that warm air rises and collects in the chamber, which can be 20°C warmer than outside. She gives birth during the harshest part of winter from late November to early January, when permanent night covers the Arctic. The cubs grow fast. Around March the mother drives two holes through the walls of the den and helps the cubs to emerge for the first time.

2 This etching shows an artist's impression of the inside of a polar bear's snow hole. The female bear gave birth to her cubs about three months ago. The cubs are now strong enough to follow their mother towards the sea where she can hunt and feed.

3 The female polar bear emerges from her winter home for the first time in the middle of March. The den's southward-facing entrance and exit hole faces towards the Sun, which is low on the horizon in early spring. The mother and her cubs are warmed by the Sun's rays.

164

Snow Homes

4 Sitting upright in a snow hollow, a female polar bear nurses her cubs. She differs from other female bears in having four working nipples rather than six. Her cubs also stay with her longer than most bears. She protects them from male bears until they are three years old. During this time she will teach her cubs how to survive in the cold Arctic conditions and also how to hunt seals.

5 On first emerging, the family remains at the den site for a few days so that the cubs become used to the cold. They play outside in the snow during the short days, and shelter in the den at night and during storms.

6 The cubs' first journey outside can be a long one. They may have to walk up to 22km to reach the sea ice where they will see their first seal hunt. The mother takes great care to avoid adult male bears who might try to kill her cubs.

Raising Cubs

Bear cubs spend the first 18 months to three years with their mother. If something should happen to her, they may be adopted by another mother with cubs the same age. The cubs learn everything from their mother. They learn to recognize the best foods and where and when to find them. They must also learn how to escape danger and how to find a winter den or shelter in a storm. Without this schooling, the young bears would not survive. Mothers and cubs can communicate by calling, particularly if they become separated or if a mother wants her offspring to follow her. During their development, cubs must keep out of the way of large male bears who might attack them.

▲ SAFE IN THE BRANCHES
Black bear cubs instinctively know that they should head for the nearest tree when danger threatens. It is easier for a mother to defend a single tree than a scattered family.

▼ MILK BAR
A mother brown bear suckles her twins. Her milk is thick and rich in fats and proteins, but low in sugars. It has three times the energy content of human or cow milk. The cubs are small at birth and must put on weight and grow quickly.

◀ LEAVING THE FAMILY

Young bears on their own, such as this brown bear, often become thin and scrawny. Despite being taught by their mothers where and how to feed, they cannot always find food. At popular feeding sites, such as fishing points, they are chased off by larger bears. When the time comes for young bears to look after themselves, the mother either chases them away or is simply not there when they return to look for her.

▶ LONG APPRENTICESHIP

Polar bear cubs are cared for by their mother for much longer than other bear cubs. They need to master the many different hunting strategies used by their mother to catch seals. These are not something that the cubs know instinctively, but rather skills that they must learn.

Did you know? Giant panda cubs are the first to leave their mothers at 18 months old

◀ FAMILY TRAGEDY

This polar bear cub is the victim in a tragic tug-of-war. A male bear has attacked the cub and its mother is trying to save it. Female polar bears fight ferociously to protect their young, but are often unsuccessful against larger opposition. Attacks like this, starvation, the cold and diseases mean that about 70 per cent of polar bear cubs do not live to their first birthday.

167

Where in the World are Bears?

Bears are found in a variety of habitats including the Arctic tundra, mountain slopes, scrub desert, temperate and tropical forests and tropical grasslands. Each species of bear, however, has its own preferred environment. The polar bear, for example, inhabits the lands and sea ice bordering the Arctic Ocean. It favours the shoreline areas where the ice breaks up and cracks appear, as this is where seals congregate. Most other bears are less specialized and have the uncanny ability to turn up wherever food is abundant. However, many of the wilderness areas where bears live are under threat. Habitat loss, as more land is cultivated for farmland and forests all over the world are cut down, is a major threat to many bears.

▲ **IN THE BAMBOO FORESTS**
The giant panda is restricted to areas of abundant bamboo forest. It was once much more widespread across eastern Asia, but now survives in just three provinces of western China – Gansu, Shanxi and Sichuan.

▼ **MOUNTAIN BEAR**
The spectacled bear lives in South America. It lives high in the Andes Mountains of Peru, Ecuador, Venezuela and Colombia. It is found in forests, including rainforests, cloud forests, and dry forests, as well as steppe (grassland) and rocky outcrops.

▲ **BROWN BEAR**
The brown bear is the most widespread of all bears. It is found in Europe, the Middle East, across Russia and northern Asia to Japan. North American brown bears live in Alaska and the Canadian Rockies.

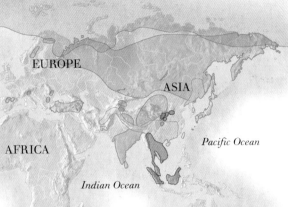

Arctic Ocean

EUROPE

NORTH AMERICA

ASIA

AFRICA

Pacific Ocean

Indian Ocean

AUSTRALIA

KEY

Asiatic black bears

Sloth bears

Sun bears

Spectacled bears

American black bears

Polar bears

Brown bears

Giant pandas

▲ BEARS OF THE WORLD

Bears are found on all continents except Africa, Australia and Antarctica. There were once brown bears living in the mountains of North Africa, but they became extinct (died out) in the 1800s.

▲ ASIATIC BLACK BEAR

The Asiatic black bear lives in mountainous regions over a wide area of southern and eastern Asia. It is found in northern India, Pakistan and on the islands of Japan and Taiwan.

▲ LIFE IN THE FOREST

The sloth bear (*above*) lives in dense, dry forests in India and Sri Lanka. The Malayan sun bear lives in similar lowland but tropical forests of South-east Asia. It is also thought to live in Yunnan in southern China, although no recent sightings have been reported.

169

Finding the Way

Bears have an uncanny knack of finding their way home even in unfamiliar territory. How they do this is only just beginning to be understood. For long distances, they rely on an ability to detect the Earth's magnetic field. This provides them with a magnetic map of their world and a compass to find their way around. When closer to home, they recognize familiar landmarks. In fact, bears have extraordinary memories, especially where food is involved. For example, a mother and her cubs are known to have trekked 32km to a favourite oak tree to feast on acorns. Five years later, the same cubs (now adults) were reported to have been seen at the same tree.

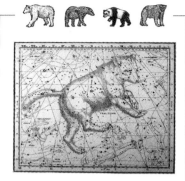

STARS IN THE SKY
The Great Bear constellation in the northern hemisphere is known to astronomers as Ursa Major. In Greek mythology, it was said to have been made in the shape of a she-bear and placed in the heavens by Zeus. The Great Bear is also worshipped in Hindu mythology as the power that keeps the heavens turning. The Inuit believe these stars represent a bear being continually chased by dogs.

▲ ARCTIC NOMADS
Polar bears are capable of swimming long distances between ice floes at speeds of up to 10km/h. They may travel thousands of kilometres across the frozen Arctic Ocean and the surrounding lands in search of prey.

▲ BAD BEAR
A sedated polar bear is transported a safe distance out of town. Nuisance bears are often moved this way but they unerringly find their way back.

GREENLAND

Baffin Island

North Western Territories

CANADA

Hudson Bay

Churchill

Quebec

Manitoba

Saskatchewan

Ontario

◄ TO AND FROM THE FOREST

The polar bears of Hudson Bay, Canada, migrate to the forests in summer and return to hunt on the sea ice in winter. On their return journey, they sometimes stop off at the town of Churchill. They gather at the rubbish dump to feed on leftovers, while they wait for ice to reform.

KEY

 Bears return to ice in winter

Bears come ashore in June and July

Bears walk north in autumn

▲ REGULAR ROUTES

Polar bears move quickly even on fast, shifting ice floes. A bear moving north, for example, against the southward-drifting ice in the Greenland Sea, can travel up to 80km in a day.

▲ HAVING KNOWLEDGE

Male brown bears live in large home ranges covering several hundred square kilometres. They must remember the locations of food and the different times of year it is available.

171

Focus on

Bears in some parts of the world are unique in terms of size or colour. Brown bears (grizzlies) on Kodiak, Shukak and Afongnak islands, Alaska, grow to a gigantic size. Across the Pacific, the brown bears of the Kamchatka Peninsula, Russia, are also giants. It is thought they reach their enormous size by including salmon as an important part of their diet.

Elsewhere, brown bears take the grizzly colour to an extreme and have fur resembling streaked hairstyles. American black bears show a very wide variation in colour. Many are not even black, ranging from white to red-brown. These variations may camouflage bears in different habitats. Black bears are invisible in dense forests, but lighter-coloured fur is an advantage in more open places.

BEAR GIANT
Standing on its hind legs, a Kodiak brown bear would tower over a person. It can weigh up to 750kg — almost as big as a North American bison. The average weight for a male Kodiak bear, however, is about 300kg. These bears are so powerful, they can kill and carry an adult moose.

CINNAMON BEAR
Cinnamon-coloured American black bears have a coat that is reddish brown to blond. Bears in the west tend to be cinnamon or honey-coloured, whereas bears in the east are mainly black.

Super Bears

BLUE BEAR
Blue or glacier black bears are found in north-west Canada. They have a blue-grey tinge to their fur. Like all American black bears, no matter what their body colour is, they have a brown muzzle.

RUSSIAN BEAR
The giant brown bears of the Kamchatka Peninsula, eastern Russia, have a varied diet. They eat the seeds of conifer trees, fish for salmon, hunt for seals and birds, and scavenge on stranded whales.

GHOST BEAR
One in ten black bears on Kermodes Island off North America's Pacific coast is snowy white. These bears are not albinos (animals that lack skin colour) or polar bears, but true black bears.

Ancient Bears

There were bears living in the past that were far bigger than today's huge Kodiak and polar bears. The giant short-faced bear, weighing over 1,000kg, was twice the size of a Kodiak. It is the largest known carnivorous (meat-eating) mammal to have ever lived on land. Bears, however, had much smaller beginnings. The first recognizable bear appeared about 20 million years ago. Called the dawn bear, it was about the size of a fox. Early bears split into three groups. The first group, the Ailuropodinae, followed a plant-based diet and of these only the giant panda still survives. The second group, Tremarctinae, included many species of short-faced bears whose only living relative today is the spectacled bear. The third group, Ursinae, includes most of the bears we see today as well as the now extinct cave bears.

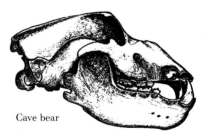

Cave bear

Brown bear

▲ BIG HEAD

The ancient cave bear (*Ursus spelaeus*) had a bigger skull than modern brown bears. Its high-domed skull anchored powerful chewing muscles. Enormous back teeth show that it mainly ate plants. It died out about 10,000 years ago.

◀ DAWN BEAR

Evolving from an animal that looked part dog, part bear and part raccoon, the dawn bear (*Ursavus elmensis*) was the ancestor of all known bears living today. Twenty million years ago it probably spent most of its time hunting in the tree-tops. By studying its teeth, scientists think the dawn bear supplemented its diet of meat with plant material and insects.

▶ GIANT SHORT-FACED BEAR

The giant short-faced bear
(*Arctodus simus*) had much
longer legs than today's bears and
probably ran down its prey. In profile it
resembled a big cat. In its jaws were canine teeth
capable of delivering a killing bite and back teeth
for shearing meat. It probably hunted ancient
camels, bison and horses that once lived on the
plains of North America. The only living
descendant of the short-faced bear is the
spectacled bear (*Tremarctos ornatus*), the sole
species of bear to be found in South America.

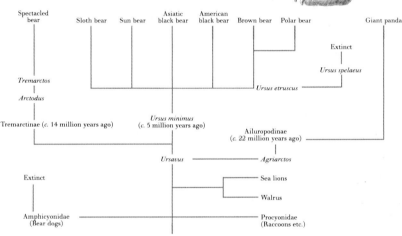

◀ FAMILY OF BEARS

This chart shows
how ancient bears
gave rise to modern
ones. The more
ancient bears are at
the bottom and
modern bears are at
the top.

◀ GREAT EUROPEAN CAVE BEAR

About 500,000 years ago, the cave
bear (*Ursus spelaeus*) evolved.
It was about the size of today's
Kodiak bears, with massive front legs,
broad paws with claws, and a huge
head and large muzzle. Large quantities
of bones found in caves throughout
Europe indicate that many died during
winter hibernation, probably because they
failed to put on enough fat to survive until spring.

175

Family Groups

The eight species of living bears belong to the family Ursidae. They all have the same general appearance, but in different parts of the world, each is adapted to a particular lifestyle. Bears in tropical places tend to be small and spend more time in the trees. Those in northern lands are larger and live mostly on the ground. To help them study bears, scientists divide the eight living species into three smaller groups, or subfamilies. The giant panda and spectacled bear are the sole survivors of two ancient subfamilies, the Ailuropodinae and Tremarctinae. The rest of the bears are grouped together in a third subfamily, the Ursinae. A bear's Latin name reveals how that particular species is grouped.

▲ **SLOTH BEAR**
Very little is known about the origins of the Indian sloth bear (*Melursus ursinus*). Few fossils (remains preserved in stone) have been found for this species of tropical bear. Sloth bears are thought to have evolved during an ice age that started about 1.6 million years ago.

◀ **BROWN BEAR**
Brown bears (*Ursus arctos*) first appeared in China about 500,000 years ago. From here they migrated right across the northern hemisphere into North America and Europe.

▲ **POLAR BEAR**
The polar bear (*Ursus maritimus*) is the most recent bear to have evolved. Its closest relative is the brown bear. In zoos, polar bears and brown bears are sometimes interbred.

▶ ASIATIC BLACK BEAR

The Asiatic black bear evolved from the same ancestor as most other species of bear, *Ursus minimus*. It is found mainly in the hilly areas of southern Russia, Japan, and southern Asia. This bear is in danger of extinction in some areas, because it is still hunted for food and medicine.

▲ GIANT PANDA

The giant panda (*Ailuropoda melanoleuca*) is the sole survivor of the earliest group of bears, the Ailuropodinae. It first appeared around 10 million years ago. Fossils of giant pandas have been found throughout China.

▼ SPECTACLED BEAR

The spectacled bear (*Tremarctos ornatus*) evolved about 2 million years ago. It is the last remaining member of a group of primitive short-faced bears (Tremarctinae) that were found mainly in the Americas.

▼ SUN BEAR

The sun bear (*Helarctos malayanus*) is another tropical bear about which very little is known. It too probably evolved during the last Ice Age. Today sun bears are under threat from pressures such as farming. The bears tear out the hearts of oil palms, which ruins the crop.

Relatives and Impostors

Bears are included in the order Carnivora, a group of mammals that includes cats, dogs and hyenas. The bears' nearest relatives are the raccoon, dog and weasel families. Bears are also probably the closest living relatives of seals and sea lions, members of the order Pinnipedia. The skull of the polar bear, for example, is very similar to that of a seal. Most relatives of bears are meat-eaters, unlike many bears themselves. Some, such as weasels, are loners, much like bears, while others, such as wolves, live in groups and hunt together. A few animals have a strong similarity to bears, but are in fact not related at all. The wombat and koala, two types of marsupial (mammals that raise their young in a pouch), are often confused with bears but are totally unrelated.

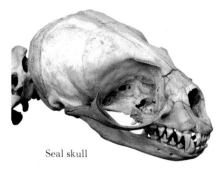

▲ **KOALA**
The Australian koala is very similar in appearance to a small bear. It is commonly called the koala bear, but it is not a bear at all. It is a more primitive mammal and is a member of the order Marsupiala. Members of this order, marsupials, have pouches in which their young develop.

◀ **RACCOON**
Raccoons have been given the name washing bear. This may be because of the way they use their front paws to locate prey. They look like they are washing their prey before eating it. Raccoons are not bears, but they are related to them.

Seal skull

▲ **ARCTIC SIMILARITIES**
Seals and bears are distant relatives. Polar bear and seal skulls have long muzzles, parallel rows of teeth and flattened bones protecting the ear.

▲ THE LONG-TAILED KINKAJOU

The kinkajou is known as the honey bear, but
it is not a real bear. It is a South American
member of the raccoon family. It spends most
of its life in the trees feeding mainly on fruit.
It is also very fond of honey. A prehensile
(grasping) tail helps it grip on to branches.

▲ DISTANT RELATIVES

Hyenas, unlike bears, live in groups in which
the females are the leaders. They have a
reputation as scavengers, but are also effective
predators. By hunting together they can bring
down large prey. Hyenas share a common early
ancestor with bears, but are actually more closely
related to cats.

▲ NO RESEMBLANCE

The weasel is a solitary carnivore, like the bear.
Stoats and weasels share the same ancestor as bears,
raccoons and dogs. However, over millions of years,
all of these animals have evolved very different
characteristics and body shapes.

▶ HUNGRY LIKE A WOLF

The grey wolf is a member of the dog family. It
often lives in the same places as brown and black
bears. It hunts in packs and sometimes targets the
same prey as bears, such as moose and caribou.

179

Pandas on the Edge

Pandas are the rarest of all bears. Each year their habitat shrinks. There are just 25 pockets of panda forest remaining, each with no more than 50 wild pandas living there. This makes pandas extremely vulnerable. One threat is the flowering of bamboo. When bamboo flowers it dies back. Each species of bamboo flowers at a different time. In the past, pandas would leave their home range and travel to where other species of bamboo were not flowering. Today, pandas are trapped by the surrounding farmland and cannot move from one bamboo stand to another. The Chinese government is desperately trying to conserve the panda. Reserves have been set up to study panda behaviour and establish breeding programmes. The panda is regarded as a national treasure. Anyone killing a panda faces the death penalty.

▲ FEEDING TIME
A baby giant panda is bottle-fed at a panda breeding centre in China. By giving the babies a helping hand early in life, it is hoped more pandas may grow to adulthood. They may then be returned to their native bamboo forests.

Did you know? Baby pandas are blind, pink and weigh just 100g at birth.

◀ CAPTIVE BREEDING
These are two of the 100 or so giant pandas in zoos and breeding centres worldwide. Unfortunately pandas are slow to have young. Artificial insemination is used in attempts to breed more pandas in captivity.

▲ SYMBOL FOR CONSERVATION

The World Wide Fund for Nature adopted the giant panda as its logo. Its rarity and universally popular appeal has made the panda a natural ambassador for all living things facing extinction.

▶ ON DISPLAY

This giant panda is far from its natural home. The chances are that it has not been bred in a zoo but taken from the wild. It is, however, safe from poachers who supply a lucrative market in panda skins.

◀ PANDA TRANSPORT

Chinese biologists in the Wolong Reserve, Sichuan, try to persuade a giant panda to enter a cage. They will move the panda to the breeding centre for further studies. It is only since the 1980s that scientists have started to understand the panda's biology.

▶ BACK TO THE WILD

Many pandas have been born in captivity, but less than a third of cubs have survived. It was hoped that captive-bred pandas could be returned to the wild, but the results are disappointing. This is because there is not enough vacant habitat to return captive pandas to. There are now 13 panda reserves and these cover about half the remaining habitat.

181

Focus on

Polar bears come into close contact with people each autumn at the isolated Canadian town of Churchill on the shores of Hudson Bay. The bears are on their way from the forests inland where they spend the summer, to the ice of the bay where they hunt. Often they arrive before the ice forms and cause a lot of trouble while they hang around with nothing to do. Some bears head for town and scare the local townsfolk. Others head for the town dump. The bears are chased away, but frequent offenders are tranquillized and transported somewhere safe. The bears, however, have become a tourist attraction. People come from all over the world to see the congregations of polar bears, which are usually much more solitary in the wild.

LOOKING FOR TROUBLE
This bear has picked up the tantalizing scent of tourists. Many visitors arrive to see the bears each year. They travel about in great buses called tundra buggies, where they are safe from the powerful and inquisitive bears.

OVERSTEPPED THE MARK
A researcher cautiously tests a tranquillized polar bear to make sure it is fully sedated. He holds a gun in case the polar bear is not as sleepy as it seems and attacks. Polar bears at Churchill occasionally threaten people. They are tranquillized and moved a safe distance away or locked up in a trap until the ice refreezes.

Churchill

BEAR BACK

A polar bear keeps cool by rolling in a patch of snow while it waits for the ice to form on Hudson Bay. The days can be warm in the Arctic autumn. Polar bears have thick fur and may overheat if they are not able to cool down.

FAST FOOD

A bear scavenges through the town rubbish dump. This is a favourite rendezvous spot. Household rubbish provides easy food for hungry bears unable to hunt.

FREE FLIGHT

A sedated bear is carried away in a net strung under a helicopter. This is a quick way to move a large animal, but it is also very expensive.

THE SIN BIN

A rogue bear is released from a bear trap. Unfortunately, bears have a well-developed homing instinct and often appear in town again. Persistent offenders are kept in a polar bear jail until the ice refreezes.

DANGER
BEAR TRAP

▲ GREAT ESCAPE

A hiker takes refuge in a tree after surprising a brown bear on a trail in Montana, USA. Adult brown bears do not climb trees. The hiker will have to wait for the bear to lose interest before he can come down.

Bears and People

Bears can be dangerous. They are attracted to food at campsites and rubbish dumps and here they come into contact with people. Fatal attacks by bears are rare. A person walking in bear country is seldom attacked, as long as the bear knows that they are there. Walkers are advised to make a lot of noise, clapping their hands and singing, for example, to warn any bears in the vicinity of their presence. Black bears tolerate people more readily than brown bears or grizzlies. Brown bears, because they have poor eyesight, might mistake people for a threat and charge. Whatever happens, a walker should never come between a mother bear and her cubs, as she will certainly fiercely defend them.

◀ BEGGING FOR FOOD

People driving in national parks in the USA offer titbits to black bears, despite warnings not to. The animals have learnt to associate cars with food. To get inside a car bears have been known to break windows or use their claws like a can-opener to slice through metal doors.

▲ BEAR WARNING

Signs warn visitors to behave sensibly. Even so, a bear might attack. It acts aggressively at first, chomping its jaws together and hitting the ground. It then charges but usually stops at the last moment.

▲ TRAPPED IN THE ZOO

A bear gnaws the bars of its tiny cage in a zoo in Tunisia. Bears are very popular animals, but they are often kept in terrible conditions in small zoos. This concrete-lined cage is totally bare and does not provide an interesting and stimulating home.

Did you know? Since 1900, there have been fewer than 150 attacks on people in the U.S.

▲ LOOKING FOR FOOD

The tempting smells coming from a dustbin are irresistible to a hungry bear. Unfortunately, bears begin to associate people with easy food. Harmless scavenging can become dangerous if the bear fails to get the food that it wants.

▲ DANGEROUS SITUATION

Bears and people cross paths occasionally. These people are too close to a brown bear for their own safety. If possible, bears should be given a wide berth. They will usually ignore or avoid people, and can be watched safely from a distance.

185

Bears in Danger

Of the eight species of bears living today, six are considered to be endangered. Only polar bears and American black bears are holding their own, and even they would not survive without considerable protection. Bears face many dangers. Their habitat is shrinking as natural areas are used to provide homes and farmland for people. Cubs are kept as pets but sold when they grow into troublesome adults. Many wild bears do not reach old age because they are shot by hunters. Hides and heads are used as wall hangings and trophies. In many parts of the world bear meat is eaten as a delicacy. Blood, bones and body parts are used in traditional Oriental medicines and as good luck charms. By far the biggest threat to bears is from poaching to supply the medicine trade.

▲ DANCING BEAR
A sloth bear is made to dance in India. Despite laws against it, bear cubs are taken from the wild. They are taught to dance using cruel methods and kept in poor conditions.

◄ BEAR CIRCUS
Bears have long been a popular act in circuses. Their ability to walk on their hind feet makes them appear almost human. These agile and clever animals are forced to perform tricks such as skipping, riding a bicycle and walking the tightrope. Performing bears are sometimes badly cared for and may be made to work all year round.

◢ ANCIENT PERSECUTION

Bears have been entertaining people for centuries. This carving from the AD300s depicts gladiators fighting bears in the arena. Both brown bears and polar bears were killed to entertain the audience.

Spinal cord treats deafness

Bones cure rheumatism

Gall bladder purifies the blood, lowers temperature and reduces inflammation

Blood cures nervousness in children

Paws prevent colds

◢ MEDICINE CHEST

Bear organs are important in Oriental medicine. The most valuable part is the gall bladder, said to cure a whole host of ailments including fevers. Many bears are killed for their gall bladder alone.

◄ HEALING

We can learn a lot from bears. Native Americans discovered that many plants eaten by bears have medicinal properties. The Cheyenne treat diarrhoea with a plant called bear's food and the Crow use bear root to cure sore throats.

► MEASURING UP

A scientist takes measurements from a tranquillized bear. A better understanding of the biology and behaviour of bears will hopefully secure them a safer future.

Whales and *Dolphins*

Robin Kerrod

Consultant: Michael Bright
BBC Natural History Unit

Whale Order

Like fish, whales and dolphins spend all their lives in the sea. But unlike fish, they breathe air, have warm blood and suckle their young. They are more closely related to human beings than fish because they are mammals. Many whales are enormous – some are as big and as heavy as a railway carriage full of passengers. Dolphins are much smaller – most are about the same size as an adult human being. Porpoises, which look much like dolphins, are also roughly the same size as humans. Although smaller, dolphins and porpoises are kinds of whales, too. All whales belong to the major group, or order, of animals called Cetacea.

▲ HEAVYWEIGHTS
The largest of the whales are the biggest animals ever to have lived. This leaping humpback whale is nearly 15m long and weighs over 25 tonnes – as much as five fully-grown elephants. Some other kinds of whales, such as the fin and blue whales, are very much bigger.

▶ WHALE ANCESTORS
More than 50 million years ago, creatures like this were swimming in the seas. They seem to have been ancestors of modern cetaceans. This creature, named basilosaurus (meaning king lizard), grew up to over 20m long. It had a snake-like body with tiny front flippers and traces of a pair of hind limbs.

▼ BALEEN WHALES
These humpback whales are feeding in Alaskan waters. They belong to the group, or suborder, of whales known as the baleen whales. These are in general very much larger than those in the other main group, the toothed whales.

Whale in the Sky

This star map shows a constellation of stars named Cetus, meaning the sea monster or whale. In Greek mythology, Cetus was a monster that was about to eat Andromeda, a maiden who had been chained to a rock as a sacrifice. Along came Perseus, who killed the sea monster and saved Andromeda.

▲ TOOTHED WHALES

A bottlenose dolphin opens its mouth and shows its teeth. It is one of the many species of toothed whales. Toothed whales have much simpler teeth than land mammals and many more of them. The bottlenose dolphin, for example, has up to 50 teeth in both its upper and lower jaws.

◀ BREATHING

Because they are mammals, whales and dolphins breathe air. This common dolphin breathes out through a blowhole on top of its head as it rises to the surface. It can hold its breath for five minutes or more when diving.

Did you know? A blue whale can weigh as much as 25 elephants.

Whales Large and Small

Most large whales belong to the major group of cetaceans called the baleen whales. Instead of teeth, these whales have brush-like plates, called baleen, that hang from their upper jaw. They use the baleen to filter food from the water. The sperm whale does not belong to the baleen group. It belongs to the other major cetacean group, called the toothed whales. This group also includes the dolphins, porpoises, white whales and beaked whales.

▲ GREY WHALE

The grey whale can grow up to nearly 15m long, and tip the scales at 35 tonnes or more. It is a similar size to the humpback, sei, bowhead and right whales, but looks quite different. Instead of the smooth skin of other whales, the grey has rough skin and no proper dorsal fin on its back.

Did you know? Some whales have as many as 3,000 baleen plates in their jaws.

▲ BLACK AND WHITE

The bowhead whale, which has a highly curved jaw, grows to 16m. It is closely related to the right whale. The bowhead is famous for its long baleen plates and thick layer of blubber. The toothed whales we call belugas *(above left)* grow to about 5m at most. The first part of the word beluga means white in Russian and belugas are also known as white whales.

▶ SEI WHALE

At up to about 16m, the sei whale looks much like its bigger relatives, the blue whale and the fin. All are members of the group called rorquals, which have deep grooves in their throat. These grooves let the throat expand to take big mouthfuls of water for feeding. Seis have up to 60 grooves in their throat.

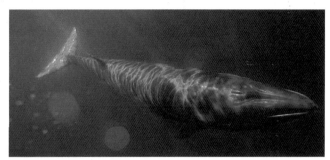

Did you know? The blue whale's tongue weighs as much as an African elephant.

▶ RELATIVE SIZES

Whales come in many sizes, from dolphins smaller than a human to the enormous blue whale, which can grow to 30m or more. In general, the baleen whales are much bigger than the toothed whales. The exception is the sperm whale, which can grow up to 18m.

porpoise

dolphin

narwhal

killer whale

beaked whale

grey whale

sperm whale

right whale

blue whale

▲ RISSO'S DOLPHIN

The dolphin pictured leaping here is a Risso's dolphin. It has a blunt snout and as few as six teeth. Most of the toothed whales that we call dolphins are on average between about 2 and 3m long. Risso's dolphins can grow a little bigger – up to nearly 4m long.

193

Whale Bones

Like all mammals, whales have a skeleton of bones to give the body its shape and protect vital organs like the heart. Because a whale's body is supported by water, its bones are not as strong as those of land mammals, and are quite soft. The backbone is made up of many vertebrae, with joints in between to give it flexibility. While providing some body support, the backbone acts mainly as an anchor for the muscles, particularly the strong muscles that drive the tail. Instead of limbs, a whale has a pair of modified fore limbs, called flippers.

◀ BONE CORSET

This advertisement for a "whalebone" corset dates from 1911, a time when women wore corsets to give them a shapely figure. The corsets were, in fact, made from the baleen plates found in whales' mouths.

▶ UNDERNEATH THE ARCHES

Arches built from the jaw bones of huge baleen whales can be seen in some ports that were once the home of whaling fleets. This jaw bone arch can be seen outside Christ Church Cathedral in Port Stanley, Falkland Islands. Nowadays, whales are protected species and building such arches is forbidden.

▶ HANDS UP

The bones in a sperm whale's flipper are remarkably similar to those in a human hand. A whale's flippers are a much changed version of a typical mammal's front limbs. Both hands have wrist bones, finger bones and joints.

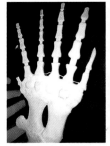

sperm whale flipper

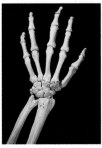

human hand

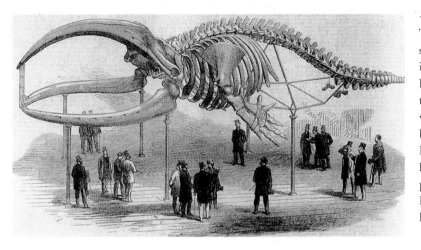

◀ BIG HEAD

This right whale skeleton was displayed in London in 1830. Its large jaw bones tell us that it is a baleen whale, which needs a big mouth for feeding. Like other mammals, it has a large rib cage to protect its body organs. However, it has no hind limbs or pelvic girdle.

▼ TOOTHY JAW

This is the skeleton of a false killer whale, one of the toothed whales. The head is much smaller than that of the baleen whales, and its jaws are studded with teeth. Its long spine is made up of segments called vertebrae. The vertebrae in the whale's waist region are large, so that they are strong enough to anchor the animal's powerful tail muscles.

Did you know? Whales are very oily and very smelly.

▼ KILLER SKULL

Both jaws of this killer whale skull are studded with vicious, curved teeth that are more than 10cm long. The killer whale is a deadly predator, attacking seals, dolphins and sometimes whales that are even bigger than itself.

Whale Bodies

Over many millions of years, whales have developed features that suit them to a life spent mostly underwater. They have long, rounded bodies and smooth, almost hairless skin. Like fish, whales move about using fins. They have the same body organs, such as heart and lungs, as land mammals. In the big whales, however, the body organs are much larger than in land mammals.

▼ BIG MOUTH

This grey whale is one of the baleen whales, and the baleen can be seen hanging from its upper jaw. Baleen whales need a big mouth so that they can take in large mouthfuls of water when they are feeding. Grey whales usually feed at the bottom of the sea.

baleen

Jonah and the Whale

This picture from the 17th century tells one of the best known of all Bible stories. The prophet Jonah was thrown overboard by sailors during a terrible storm. To rescue him, God sent a whale, which swallowed him whole. Jonah spent three days in the whale's belly before it coughed him up on to dry land. The picture shows that many people at this time had little idea of what a whale looked like. The artist has given it shark-like teeth and a curly tail.

▼ LEAPING DOLPHINS

A pair of bottlenose dolphins leap effortlessly several metres out of the water. Powerful muscles near the tail provide them with the energy for fast swimming and leaping. They leap for various reasons – to signal to each other, to look for fish or perhaps just for fun.

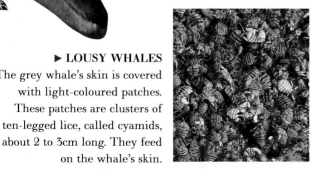

► LOUSY WHALES

The grey whale's skin is covered with light-coloured patches. These patches are clusters of ten-legged lice, called cyamids, about 2 to 3cm long. They feed on the whale's skin.

▲ HANGERS ON

This humpback whale's throat is covered with barnacles, which take hold because the whale moves quite slowly. They cannot easily cling to swifter-moving cetaceans, such as dolphins. A dolphin sloughs rough skin away as it moves through the water. This also makes it harder for a barnacle to take hold.

◄ BODY LINES

A pod, or group, of melon-headed whales swim in the Pacific Ocean. This species is one of the smaller whales, at less than 3m long. It shows the features of a typical cetacean – a well-rounded body with a short neck and a single fin. It has a pair of paddle-like front flippers and a tail with horizontal flukes.

Did you know? Whales have whiskers on their faces.

197

Staying Alive

Whales are warm-blooded creatures. To stay alive, they must keep their bodies at a temperature of about 36–37°C. They swim in very cold water that quickly takes heat away from the surface of their bodies. To stop body heat reaching the surface, whales have a thick layer of fatty blubber just beneath the skin. Whales must also breathe to stay alive. They breathe through a blowhole, situated on top of the head. When a whale breathes out, it sends a column of steamy water vapour high into the air.

▲ **IN THE WARM**
Southern right whales feed in icy Antarctic waters in summer. The whales' size helps limit the percentage of body heat they lose to the water.

epidermis

blood vessels

layer of blubber

◄ **SKIN DEEP**
This is a cross-section of a whale's outer layer. Beneath its skin, a thick layer of blubber insulates it from ice-cold water.

▶ **SMALL BODY**
Atlantic spotted dolphins are about the size of a human. Because it is small, its body has a relatively large surface area for its size and so loses heat faster than its big relatives. This is probably why the Atlantic spotted dolphin lives in quite warm waters.

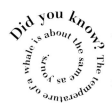

Did you know? The temperature of a whale is about the same as yours.

► SKY HIGH
A humpback whale surfaces and blows a column of warm, moist air. As it rises it cools, and the moisture in it condenses into a cloud of tiny water droplets.

▼ DEEP DIVING
Whales feed at different depths. Most dolphins feed close to the surface. The sperm whale holds the diving record, being able to descend to about 2,000m and stay under water for up to an hour.

Depth		Length of Dive
Surface		common dolphin 15 minutes
600m		fin whale 20 minutes
		pilot whale 15 minutes
1200m		
1800m		
		sperm whale 60 minutes
2400m		

▼ ONE BLOWHOLE
Like all toothed whales, a bottlenose dolphin has only one blowhole. When the dolphin dives, thick lips of elastic tissue close it to stop water entering, no matter how deep the dive.

▲ TWO BLOWHOLES
The humpback whale breathes out through a pair of blowholes, located behind a ridge called a splashguard. This helps prevent water entering the blowholes when the whale is blowing.

199

Whale Brain and Senses

A whale controls its body through its nervous system. The brain is the control centre, carrying out functions automatically, but also acting upon information supplied by the senses. The sizes of whale brains varies, according to the animal's size. However, dolphins have much bigger brains for their size. Hearing is by far a whale's most important sense. They pick up sounds with tiny ears located just behind the eyes.

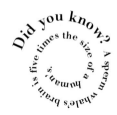

▲ EYES
Compared with its large body, a whale's eyes are tiny. It can see quite well when it is on the surface and often lifts its head out of the water to look around.

Did you know? A sperm whale's brain is five times the size of a human's.

◀ CLOSE ENCOUNTERS
A group of Atlantic spotted dolphins swim closely together in the seas around the Bahama Islands. Like most other cetaceans, the dolphins often nudge one another and stroke each other with their flippers and tail. Touch plays a very important part in dolphin society, especially in courtship.

◄ SLAP HAPPY

A humpback whale slapping its tail, or lob-tailing, a favourite pastime for great whales. Lob-tailing creates a noise like a gunshot in the air, but, more importantly, it will make a loud report underwater. All the other whales in the area will be able to hear the noise.

Cupids and Dolphins

In this Roman mosaic, cupids and dolphins gambol together. In Roman mythology, Cupid was the god of love. Roman artists were inspired by the dolphin's intelligence and gentleness. They regarded them as sacred creatures.

◄ BRAINY
DOLPHIN?

Some dolphins, such as the bottlenose, have a brain that is much the same size as our own. It is quite a complex brain with many folds. However, the dolphin is not necessarily highly intelligent.

► IN TRAINING

A bottlenose dolphin is shown with its trainer. This species has a particularly large brain for its size. It can be easily trained and has a good memory. It can observe other animals and learn to mimic their behaviour in a short space of time. It is also good at solving problems, something we consider a sign of intelligence.

Sounds and Songs

Whales use sounds to communicate with one another, and to find their food. Baleen whales use low-pitched sounds, which have been picked up by underwater microphones as moans, grunts and snores. The toothed whales make higher-pitched sounds, picked up as squeaks, creaks or whistles. Whales also use high-pitched clicks when hunting. They send out beams of sound, which are reflected by objects in their path, such as fish. The whale picks up the reflected sound, or echo, and works out the object's location. This is called echo-location.

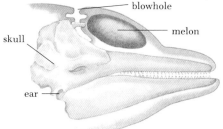

blowhole

melon

skull

ear

◄ ECHO SOUNDINGS
The Amazon river dolphin hunts by echo-location. It sends out up to 80 high-pitched clicks per second. The sound transmits in a beam from a bulge on top of its head. All toothed whales and dolphins hunt in this way.

► SEA CANARIES
A group of belugas, or white whales, swim in a bay in Canada. Belugas' voices can clearly be heard above the surface. This is why they are known as sea canaries. They also produce high-pitched sounds we cannot hear, which they use for echo-location.

▲ MAKING WAVES
A dolphin vibrates the air in its nasal passages to make high-pitched sound waves, which are focused into a beam by the melon – a bulge on its head. The sound beam transmits into the water.

◄ SUPER SONGSTER

This male humpback whale is heading for the breeding grounds where the females are gathering. The male starts singing long and complicated songs. This may be to attract a mate, or to warn other males off its patch. The sound can carry for 30km or more.

▼ LONG SONGS

This is a voice print of a humpback whale's song, picked up by an underwater microphone. It shows complex musical phrases and melodies. Humpback whales often continue singing for a day or more, repeating the same song.

▼
SOUND ECHOES

A sperm whale can locate a giant squid more than a kilometre away by transmitting pulses of sound waves into the water and listening. The echo is picked up by the teeth in its lower jaw and the vibrations are sent along the jaw to the ear.

Did you know? A dolphin picks up sounds through its lower jaw.

◄ ALIEN GREETINGS

The songs of the humpback whale not only travel through Earth's oceans, but they are also travelling far out into Space. They are among the recorded typical sounds of our world that are being carried by the two Voyager space probes. These probes are now many millions of kilometres away from Earth and are on their way to the stars.

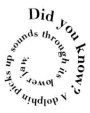

203

Feeding Habits

▲ **CRUNCHY KRILL**
These crustaceans, known as krill, form the diet of many baleen whales. Measuring up to 75mm long, they swim in vast shoals, often covering an area of several square kilometres. Most krill are found in Antarctic waters.

Most baleen whales feed by taking mouthfuls of seawater containing fish and tiny shrimp-like creatures called krill or plankton, as well as algae, jellyfish, worms and so on. The whale closes its mouth and lifts its tongue, forcing water out through the bristly baleen plates on the upper jaw. The baleen acts like a sieve and holds back the food, which the whale then swallows. Toothed whales feed mainly on fish and squid. They find their prey by echo-location.

◄ **PLOUGHING**
A grey whale ploughs into the seabed, stirring up sand and ooze. It dislodges tiny crustaceans, called amphipods, and gulps them down. Grey whales feed mostly in summer in the Arctic before they migrate south.

◄ **SKIM FEEDING**
With its mouth open, a southern right whale filters tiny crustaceans, called copepods, out of the water with its baleen. It eats up to two tonnes of these plankton daily. It eats so much because of its huge size – up to 80 tonnes. Usually right whales feed alone, but if food is plentiful, several will feed cruising side by side.

◄ SUCCULENT SQUID

Squid is the sperm whale's favourite food and is eaten by other toothed whales and dolphins as well. Squid are molluscs, in the same animal order as snails and octopuses. Unlike octopuses, they have eight arms and two tentacles, and are called decapods (meaning ten feet). Squid swim together in dense shoals, many thousand strong.

◄ TOOTHY SMILE

A Ganges river dolphin has more than 100 teeth. The front ones are very long. Ganges river dolphins eat mainly fish, and also take shrimp and crab. They usually feed at night and find their prey by echo-location.

Did you know? A blue whale eats nearly 1,000kg of krill in a single meal.

► LUNCH

Belugas feed on squid and small fish, which are in plentiful supply in the icy ocean. Unlike common dolphins, belugas do not have many teeth. They may simply suck prey into their mouths. Many beaked whales, which also feed on squid, have no teeth suitable for clutching prey.

▲ HUNT THE SQUID

The sperm whale is the largest toothed whale, notable for its huge head and tiny lower jaw. It hunts the giant squid that live in waters around 2,000m deep. At that depth, in total darkness, it hunts its prey by echo-location.

Focus on

Among the toothed whales, the killer whale, or orca, is the master predator. It feeds on a wider variety of prey than any other whale. It bites and tears its prey to pieces with its fearsome teeth and may also batter them with its powerful tail. It is the only whale to take warm-blooded prey. Fortunately, there is no record of a killer whale ever attacking human beings. As well as fish and squid, a killer whale will hunt seals, penguins, dolphins and porpoises. It may even attack large baleen whales many times its size. Killer whales live in family groups, or pods. They often go hunting together, which greatly improves the chance of success.

1 A killer whale will go hunting by itself if it chances upon a likely victim, such as this lone sea lion. This hungry whale has spotted the sea lion splashing in the surf at the water's edge. With powerful strokes of its tail, it surges towards its intended prey. The whale's tall dorsal fin shows that it is a fully-grown male.

2 The sea lion seems totally unaware of what is happening but, in any case, it is nearly helpless in the shallow water. The killer whale is scraping the shore as it homes in for the kill.

Killer Whales

3 Suddenly the killer's head bursts out of the water, and its jaws gape open. Its vicious teeth, curving inwards and backwards, are exposed. It is ready to sink them into its sea lion prey. The killer whale may have fewer teeth than most toothed whales, but they are large and very strong.

4 Now the killer snaps its jaws shut, clamping the sea lion in a vice-like grip. With its prey struggling helplessly, it slides back into deep water to eat its fill. Killer whales sometimes almost beach themselves when they lunge after prey but, helped by the surf, they usually manage to wriggle their way back into the sea.

The humpback whale usually scoops up water as it lunges forwards and upwards to feed. Grooves in its throat lets the mouth expand to take in tonnes of water containing food, which it filters through its baleen plates. This way of lunge-feeding is typical of the baleen whales known as the rorquals, which also include the blue, fin, sei and minke whales. Before lunge-feeding, humpbacks may blow a circle of bubbles around the fish. The bubbles act like a net to stop the fish escaping.

ON THE LOOKOUT
A humpback whale spy-hops in the feeding grounds of Alaska. It is looking for signs of shoals of fish, such as cod. In the Northern Hemisphere, humpbacks feed mainly on fish. The Southern Hemisphere humpbacks feed mainly on plankton, such as krill.

FORWARD LUNCE
Once in the middle of a shoal, the humpback opens its mouth and lunges forwards. The throat grooves expand as water rushes in. It uses its tongue and cheek muscles to force the water through its baleen plates, leaving the fish behind in its mouth.

Lunging for Lunch

UPWARD LUNGE

Here, the humpback is using a different technique. It sinks below the surface and then flicks its tail to help it to shoot upwards again. With mouth gaping open, it lunges at the fish from below.

RING OF BUBBLES

The surface of the sea is boiling with a ring of frothy bubbles. Unseen, beneath the water, one or more humpback whales swim in circles, letting out air as they do so.

BUBBLE NETTING

The circle of bubbles rises to the surface from the whales circling under the water. It forms a kind of net around a shoal of fish. The whales then swim up to the surface, mouths gaping, to engulf the netted prey.

209

Swimming

All whales are superb swimmers. All parts of the whale's body help it move through the water. The driving force comes from the tail fin, or flukes. Using very powerful muscles in the rear third of its body, the whale beats its tail up and down and the whole body bends. It uses its pectoral fins, or flippers, near the front of the body to steer with. The body itself is streamlined and smooth to help it slip through the water easily. The body can change shape slightly to keep the water flowing smoothly around it. Little ridges under the skin help as well.

▲ STEERING

Among whales, the humpback has by far the longest front flippers. As well as for steering, it uses its flippers for slapping the water. Flipper-slapping seems to be a form of communication.

◄ TAIL POWER

The tail flukes of a grey whale rise into the air before it dives. Whales move their broad tails up and down to drive themselves through the water.

▼ MASSIVE FIN

The dorsal fin of a killer whale projects high into the air. The animal is a swift swimmer, and the fin helps keep its body well balanced. The killer whale has such a large dorsal fin that some experts believe it may help to regulate their body temperature, or even be used in courtship. Most whales and dolphins have a dorsal fin, although some only have a raised hump.

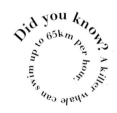

Did you know? A killer whale can swim up to 65km per hour.

◄ STREAMLINING
Atlantic spotted dolphins' bodies are beautifully streamlined – shaped so that they slip easily through the water when they move. The dolphin's body is long and rounded, broad in front and becoming narrower towards the tail. Apart from the dorsal fin and flippers, nothing projects from its body. It has no external ears or rear limbs.

▼ HOW A DOLPHIN SWIMS
Dolphins beat their tail flukes up and down by means of the powerful muscles near the tail. The flukes force the water backwards at each stroke. As the water is forced back, the dolphin's body is forced forwards. Its other fins help guide it through the water. They do not provide propulsion.

◄ SMOOTH SKINNED
This bottlenose dolphin is tailwalking – supporting itself by powerful thrusts of its tail. Unlike most mammals, it has no covering of hair or hair follicles – the dimples in the skin from which the hair grows. Its smooth skin helps the dolphin's body slip through the water.

▼ HOW A FISH SWIMS
It is mainly the tail that provides the power for a fish to swim. The tail has vertical fins, unlike the horizontal fins of the dolphin. It swims by beating its tail and body from side to side.

211

Focus on

Most whales feed beneath the surface, some often diving deep to reach their food. We can usually identify the species of whale from the way it prepares to dive, or sound. The sperm whale, for example, is one of the species that lifts its tail high into the air before it descends into the ocean. It is the deepest diver of all the whales, sometimes descending to more than a kilometre in search of squid. It can stay under water for an hour or more before it has to come up for air. As in other whales, its lungs collapse when it dives. It is thought that the great mass of oil in its head helps the whale when diving and surfacing.

1 Two sperm whales swim at the surface. The one on the right is preparing to dive. Its head is in the air, and it fills its lungs with air in a series of blows. The sperm whale's blow projects forwards, as in no other whale.

2 The diving whale lashes its tail and accelerates through the water, creating a foaming wake. Now the whale starts the dive, thrusting its bulbous head down and arching its back steeply. The rounded hump on its back rises high into the air. The lumpy knuckles behind the hump become visible as the body arches over.

Diving

3 As the whale's head goes under, the oil in its head freezes and becomes heavier on the way down, then melts and becomes lighter again on the way up. If it is going to make a deep dive, the whale may not take another breath for more than an hour.

4 Soon the body disappears with just the tail flukes poking out of the water. The body is now in a vertical position and that is how it remains as the whale dives swiftly into the deep. Descending at speeds of more than 150m per minute, it is soon in darkness, scanning its surroundings by beams of sound for the squid on which it feeds.

Social Life

Every day we meet, work, play and communicate with other people. We are sociable animals. Some whales are also sociable and live together. Sperm whales live in groups of up to about 50. A group may be a breeding school of females and young or a bachelor school of young males. Older male sperm whales live alone, except in the breeding season. Beluga whales often live in groups of several hundred. Baleen whales are not as sociable. They move singly or in small groups, probably because of their huge appetite – they could not find enough food if they lived close together.

▲ HERD INSTINCT
Beluga whales gather together in very large groups, or herds, and they mostly stay in these herds for life. Many of the animals in this group, pictured in the Canadian Arctic, have calves. These can be recognized, not only by their smaller size, but also by their darker skin colour.

Did you know? Dolphins will nudge a sick member of the group up to the surface, so it does not drown.

▼ NOSEY ORCAS
Two killer whales, or orcas, spy-hop in Antarctic waters. They rise out of the water together, as if on a signal. They are members of the same pod, which stay together all their lives. The bonds between the animals are very strong. This helps them coordinate their activities, especially when hunting for food.

Did you know? Male whales often try to help injured females. Females rarely try to help injured males.

◄ STAYING CLOSE

Two Atlantic spotted dolphins swim with their young. The young's spots will not start to appear until the animals are about a year old. As with many other species, the young stay very close to their parents most of the time.

▼ HUMAN CONTACT

A bottlenose dolphin swims alongside a boy. These dolphins live in social groups but lone outcasts, or animals that have become separated from their group, often approach humans.

▲ SOLITARY SWIMMER

An Amazon river dolphin rests on the river bed. It spends most of its life alone, or with just one other. This solitary behaviour is typical of river dolphins, but untypical of most whales and ocean dolphins.

► PILOT ERROR

These long-finned pilot whales are stranded on a beach. Pilot whales usually live in large groups, with strong bonds between group members. One whale may strand itself on a beach. The others may try to help it and get stranded, too. themselves.

The Mating Game

Whales mate at certain times of year. Baleen whales mate during the late autumn after the whales have migrated to their warm-water breeding grounds. One whale will mate a number of times with different partners. Several males may attempt to manoeuvre a female into a mating position. Often the males fight each other for the chance to mate. Male narwhals even fence with their long tusks. But mating behaviour can also be gentle, with the males and females caressing one another with their flippers.

▲ **WHITE WEDDING**
A pair of belugas show interest in each other. Males and females spend the year in separate groups, only mixing in the mating season. They mate and calve in bays in the far north.

◄ **LOVE SONG**
Whales attract mates by body language and sound. This humpback can pinpoint another's position, and perhaps exchange messages, over great distances.

◄ **MATING TIFFS**
Two grey whales court in the winter breeding grounds off Baja California, Mexico. Usually, a group of males fights for the right to mate with a female, causing commotion in the water. The female might mate many times with them.

◄ ROLLOVER
Courtship for these southern right whales is nearly over. The male *(top)* has succeeded in getting the female to roll over on her back and is moving into the mating position.

The Fabulous Unicorn

In the breeding season, male narwhals fight each other using their long tusks, which often break. Long ago, when these small whales were little known, people found the tusks and wondered what kind of creature they came from. This may have led to the idea of the unicorn, a horse-like beast with a long spiral horn (like the narwhal's) on its forehead.

◄ BELLY TO BELLY
A pair of southern right whales mate, belly to belly. The male has inserted his long penis into the female to inject his sperm. Usually, the male's penis stays hidden in the body behind a genital slit. It will be nine months or more before the female gives birth to a single calf.

▼ BIG BABY
A sperm whale calf snuggles up to its mother. A calf might measure up to 4.5m long when born, nearly 15 months after mating took place. The mother feeds it for a year or more, leaving it only to dive deep for food.

Did you know? Female sperm whales can mate at the age of 8. Males cannot mate until they are nearly 20.

217

Focus on

BIRTHDAY
A bottlenose dolphin gives birth. The baby is born tail-first. This birth is taking place near the bottom of an aquarium. In the wild, birth takes place close to the surface so the baby can surface quickly and start breathing.

After mating, the female whale becomes pregnant and a baby whale starts to grow inside her body. After about a year, the calf is ready to be born. By now it can weigh, in the case of the blue whale, up to 2.5 tonnes. The first thing the calf must do is take a breath, and the mother or another whale may help it to the surface. Soon it finds one of the mother's nipples to suck the rich milk in her mammary glands (breasts). It suckles for several months until it learns to take solid food such as fish. Mother and calf may spend most of the time alone, or join nursery schools with other mothers and calves.

SUCKLING
A beluga mother suckles her young under water. Her fatty milk is very nutritious, and the calf grows rapidly. It will drink milk for up to two years. At birth the calf's body is dark grey, but it slowly lightens as the calf matures.

Bringing Up Baby

Did you know? The calves of baleen whales stop breast feeding after about 9 months – much sooner than toothed whale calves.

AT PLAY

A young Atlantic spotted dolphin and its mother play together, twisting, turning, rolling and touching each other with their flippers. During play, the young dolphin learns the skills it will need later in life when it has to fend for itself. The youngster is darker than its mother and has no spots. These do not start to appear until it is about a year old.

TOGETHERNESS

A humpback whale calf sticks closely to its mother as she swims slowly in Hawaiian waters. The slipstream, or water flow, created by the mother's motion helps pull it along. For the first few months of its life, it will not stray far from its mother's side.

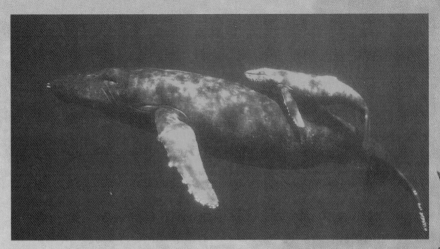

Having Fun

Dolphins have long delighted people with their acrobatic antics. They somersault, ride the bow waves of boats and go surfing. Dusky and spinner dolphins are particularly lively. Some antics have a purpose, such as sending signals to other dolphins. But often the animals seem to perform just for fun. In most animal species only the young play. In whale and dolphin society, adults play too. Southern right whales play a sailing game. They hang in the water with their heads down and tails in the air. The tails act like sails and catch the wind, and they are blown along.

▲ PLAYFUL PAIR

Two Atlantic spotted dolphins jostle as they play with a sea fan. Dolphins spend much of their time playing, especially the younger ones. They make up games, using anything they can find. Their games can last for hours.

▼ JUMPING FOR JOY

A pair of bottlenose dolphins leaps high, leaving the water together, as if they have rehearsed their act. They seem to jump for joy, but their behaviour may have a social function within their family group.

► **PORPOISING ON PURPOSE**

A group of long-snouted spinner dolphins go porpoising, taking long, low leaps as they swim. They churn the water behind them into a foam. Many dolphins practise porpoising, in order to travel fast on the surface.

Did you know? Killer whales like brushing against each other as they swim at high speed.

◄ **RIDING THE WAKE**

A Pacific white-sided dolphin surfs the waves. This is one of the most acrobatic of the dolphins. It is often seen bow-riding in front of boats. Other species of dolphins also like to ride in the waves left in the wake of passing boats.

Did you know? The rough skin on a porpoise's back may be for giving calves piggy-backed rides.

► **AQUATIC ACROBAT**

This dusky dolphin is throwing itself high into the air. It twists and turns, spins and performs somersaults. This behaviour is like a roll call – to check that every dolphin in the group is present and ready to go hunting. The behaviour is repeated after hunting to gather the group together once more.

Did you know? A dolphin may play cat and mouse with its prey before eating it.

Focus on

A whale leaps from the sea and crashes back to the surface in a shower of spray. This activity, called breaching, is common among humpbacks. Some may breach up to 200 times in succession. When one animal starts breaching, others follow suit. Whales put on other displays as well, including slapping their flippers and tail on the surface. These activities could, like breaching, be some form of signalling. Spy-hopping is another activity, often done to look for signs of fish to eat.

BREACHING

Propelled by powerful thrusts of its tail, the humpback launches its vast bulk into the air, twisting as it does so. For a creature weighing up to 30 tonnes, this is no mean feat. As breaching ends, it crashes back to the surface with a splash. This time it lands on its back, with one of its flippers up in the air.

FLIPPER-FLOPPING

The humpback swims on the surface, raising one flipper in the air. It rolls over and slaps the flipper on the water several times, perhaps to warn off rivals. Its flipper-flopping is noisy because its flippers are so large.

Whales on Display

WHAT A FLUKE!

The humpback raises its tail in the air during the display known as lob-tailing or tail-slapping. The tail is also exposed when the whale is about to dive, behaviour called fluking. It is easy to tell if a humpback is lob-tailing or fluking. In fluking, the tail disappears below the surface quietly.

LOB-TAILING

In lob-tailing, the tail slaps on the water with a noise like a gunshot. The only other time a humpback shows its flukes is when it is about to go on a deep dive.

SPY-HOPPING

The humpback on the right of the picture is spy-hopping. It positions itself vertically in the water and pokes out its head until its eyes are showing. Then it has a good look round. The other humpback here is doing the opposite, poking out its tail, ready to lob-tail.

Where Whales are Found

Whales are found in all the world's oceans. Some range widely, while others are found only in a certain area. They may stay in the same place all year long, or migrate from one area to another with the seasons. Some whales stick to shallow coastal areas, others prefer deep waters. Some live in the cool northern or southern parts of the world. Others are more at home in tropical regions near the Equator. Some species even live in rivers.

◄ OCEAN WANDERER

A humpback whale surfaces to blow while swimming at Cape Cod off the north-east coast of North America. In winter, the humpback feeds in high latitudes. It migrates to low latitudes to breed during the summer.

▲ MUDDY WATERS

The mud-laden waters of the River Amazon in South America are the habitat of the Amazon river dolphin. Here, one shows off its teeth. This species ranges along the Amazon and its tributaries.

Did you know? Some dolphins come and go between salt water and fresh water.

◄ WORLDWIDE KILLER

Among ice-floes in the Arctic Ocean, a killer whale hunts for prey. Killer whales are found in all the oceans. They live in coastal areas but may venture out to the open ocean. They also swim inshore among the surf, and may beach to snatch their prey.

▶ SNOW WHITE

These belugas, or white whales, are in Hudson Bay, Canada. These cold-water animals live around coasts in the far north of North America, Europe and Asia. They venture into estuaries and even up rivers. In winter they hunt in the pack ice in the Arctic.

◀ TROPICAL MELONS

A pod of melon-headed whales is shown swimming in the Pacific Ocean. These creatures prefer warm waters and are found in subtropical and tropical regions in both the Northern and Southern Hemispheres. They generally stay in deep water, keeping well away from land.

▶ WIDE RANGER

A bottlenose dolphin lunges through the surf in the sunny Bahamas. This animal is one of the most wide-ranging of the dolphins, being found in temperate to tropical waters in both the Northern and Southern Hemispheres. It is also found in enclosed seas such as the Mediterranean and Red Sea. Mostly it stays in coastal waters. When bottlenose dolphins migrate to warmer areas, they lose weight. When they return to colder climes, their blubber increases again.

Migration

Grey whales spend the summer months feeding in the Arctic Ocean. Many of the females are pregnant. Before winter comes, the whales head south towards Mexico for warmer waters, where the females will give birth to their calves. In the warmer climate, the calves stand a better chance of surviving. Mating takes place around late summer. When spring comes, the greys head north to the Arctic. Their annual journey between feeding and breeding grounds involves a round trip of some 20,000km. The humpbacks take part in long migrations too. Most of the other large rorquals and the right whales seem to undergo similar migrations.

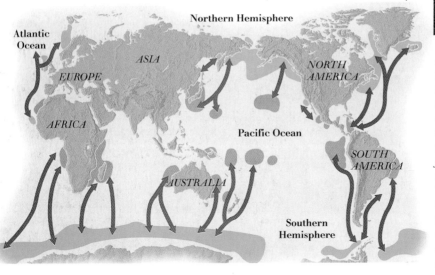

Migration
This map shows the routes taken by humpback whales during their annual migrations between their summer feeding and winter breeding grounds. There are at least three main groups, two in the Northern and one in the Southern Hemisphere.

KEY TO MAP

breeding grounds	feeding grounds

◄ SUMMER FEEDING
Two Southern Hemisphere humpbacks feed in the Antarctic Ocean during the summer months. This is when the krill and other plankton they feed on thrive. The whales have taken huge mouthfuls of water, which they sieve for plankton using the baleen on their upper jaws.

▼ RIGHT LOCATION

The tail fluke of a southern right whale is thrust into the air as the whale sails. This whale is one of a group of right whales in winter breeding grounds off the coast of Argentina. By summer the whales will have returned south to feed in the Antarctic Ocean.

Did you know? Grey whales make longer migrations than any other mammal.

▲ WINTER BREEDING

It is early winter and two humpbacks have migrated north from the Antarctic to a shallow bay on the coast of eastern Australia. A large group of humpbacks will mate here and, about 12 months later, the females will give birth.

▼ MATING GREYS

In the winter breeding grounds of Baja California, a grey whale surfaces. They spend about three months in the region, where mating and (two years later) births take place.

High and Dry

Dead whales are often found washed up, or stranded, on the seashore. Live whales are sometimes found too, particularly open ocean species, such as sperm whales. Some live whales probably strand when they become ill. Others strand when they lose their sense of direction. Whales are thought to find their way using the Earth's magnetism as a kind of map. Any change in the magnetism may cause them to turn the wrong way and head for the shore. Mass strandings also take place, with scores of whales left helpless. This happens particularly among sociable species, such as the pilot whales.

Did you know? When people help stranded whales, the whales often swim back and get stranded again.

▲ BEACHED DOLPHIN
This Atlantic white-sided dolphin is stranded on a beach in the Orkney Islands. The dolphins usually travel in big groups, so mass strandings occur too.

▲ WAITING FOR THE TIDE
People come to the aid of stranded long-finned pilot whales in New Zealand. They cover the whales to prevent sunburn and throw water over them to keep their skin moist.

◄ RARE STRANDING

Marine biologists examine a stranded Stejneger's beaked whale. Beaked whales are among the least known of all the cetaceans. Most of our knowledge about them comes from occasional strandings. Several beaked whales, such as this one, have a large tooth protruding from the jaws.

Did you know? Whales stranded in Britain belong to the monarch.

► IN THE SHALLOWS

Three belugas became stranded in shallow water as the tide went out. Polar bears may attack when they are beached. Belugas rarely become stranded, and usually survive until the tide comes in again.

▼ BIG FIN

A huge fin whale has become beached on a mudflat. This animal is dead, but even if it were alive, it would be impossible to return to the water. When a whale of this size is not supported by water its internal organs collapse. Scientists examine stranded bodies to learn about whales.

Grey and Right Whales

Grey whales and the three species of right whale, including the bowhead, are all filter-feeders with baleen plates in their upper jaws. The bowhead has the longest baleen of all, while the grey whale has short baleen. Unlike most baleen whales, the grey whale feeds mainly on the seabed. It is found only in the Northern Hemisphere, but there are right whales in both hemispheres. Right whales were named by whalers because they were the right whales to catch for their high yields of oil and baleen. They swam slowly, they could be approached easily and floated when dead.

▲ MOTTLED MAMMAL
The long, narrow head of a grey whale breaks the surface. Its closed blowholes are in the middle of the picture. The head is covered here and there with clusters of barnacles and lice. This, together with lighter body patches, gives the animal a mottled appearance.

▲ WHITE CHIN
A bowhead whale thrusts its head out of the water, exposing its unique white chin, covered with black patches. The skin is smooth, with no growths like those on the skin of the northern and southern right whales.

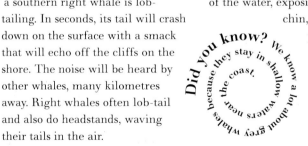

◀ LIVELY LOB
Near the coast of Argentina in South America, a southern right whale is lob-tailing. In seconds, its tail will crash down on the surface with a smack that will echo off the cliffs on the shore. The noise will be heard by other whales, many kilometres away. Right whales often lob-tail and also do headstands, waving their tails in the air.

Did you know? We know a lot about grey whales because they stay in shallow waters near the coast.

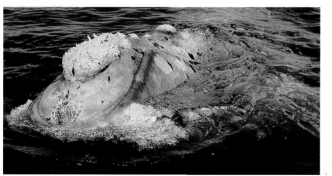

◄ BEARDED

A southern right whale cruises in the South Atlantic. One distinctive feature of this whale is the deeply curved jawline. Another is its beard and bonnet. These are large growths on the whale's chin and nose, which become infested with barnacles.

◄ HAIRY MONSTER

The northern right whale lives in the North Atlantic. Whalers used to call the crusty hard skin on its head a bonnet or rock garden. Lice and barnacles live on this skin, which can grow enormous. Right whales are the hairiest of all whales, keeping more hair after birth than other cetaceans. It even grows facial hair!

Did you know? You can tell a grey whale by its unique long, very narrow head.

► BRISTLY JAWS

A grey whale opens its mouth, showing the baleen plates on its upper jaw. The baleen is quite short, stiff and coarse. The whale uses it to filter out the tiny creatures it digs out of the seabed when feeding. Grey whales are not shy and sometimes swim up to the boats of whale-watchers.

Rorquals

The rorquals are a
family of baleen
whales that includes the
largest creature ever to live, the
blue whale. They are named
after the grooves on their throat — the
word rorqual means a furrow. All rorquals,
except the humpback, have a long streamlined body with a sharp nose and a
dorsal fin set well back. They can swim at up to 30kph. The humpback is a
slower swimmer with a chunkier body. It has knobbly flippers and a hump in
front of the dorsal fin. It is famous for the songs it sings. The minke whale is the
smallest rorqual. Bryde's whale lives mainly in tropical and subtropical waters,
while the other rorquals often venture into colder waters as well, often
venturing into polar waters in the summer.

▼ **TINY MINKE**
The minke whale grows to only about one-third
of the size of the blue whale and never exceeds
10 tonnes in weight. It has a slim snout and a
curved dorsal fin. Its flippers are short and
can be marked with a
broad white band.

▲ **WHALE WITH A HUMP**
This picture of a humpback whale shows the feature that
gives it its name very well. Its small dorsal
fin sits on top of a pronounced hump on
its back. This profile view of the animal
also shows the prominent splash guard
on its head in front of the blowholes.

Did you know? humpback whales can live to age 95.

▼ **KNOBBLY FLIPPER**
A humpback whale swims
on the surface, with one of
its flippers up in the air
like a boat sail. The flippers
of the humpback are by far
the most distinctive of all
the whales. They are sturdy
and very
long —
up to a
third of the
length of the
whale's body. The
flippers have knobs
along their front edge.

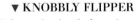
flipper

◀ BIG GULP

A blue whale feeds in Californian waters. It has taken in a mouthful of water containing thousands of the tiny shrimp-like krill it feeds on. The grooves on its throat that allow its mouth to expand can be clearly seen. A blue whale typically has between 60 and 90 of these grooves.

▶ DRIPPING FLUKES

A blue whale fluking, with its tail flukes rising out of the water before the animal dives. Among rorquals, only blue and humpback whales expose their flukes before diving. The humpback's tail flukes are quite different. They are knobbly at the rear edges and have white markings on the underside.

Did you know? A blue whale's heart is about the size of a small car.

◀ SEI WHALE

The sei whale can be found in most of the oceans. It feeds in the cool Arctic or Antarctic waters during the summer and migrates to warmer waters in the winter to breed. With a length of up to about 18m, it is slightly larger than the similar looking Bryde's whale.

233

Sperm and White Whales

The sperm and the white whales are two families of toothed whales. The sperm whale and dwarf and pygmy sperm whales have an organ in their head called the spermaceti organ, which is filled with wax. The wax may help the animals when they dive and may play a part in focusing the sound waves they use for echo-location. The sperm whale and the two white whales (the beluga and the narwhal) have no dorsal fin. The sperm whale has teeth only on its lower jaw. The beluga has up to 20 teeth in each of its jaws, but the narwhal has only two. In the male narwhal, one of the teeth grows into a long spiral tusk, measuring up to 3m.

◀ BABY EYES
The eye of a sperm whale calf. Like all whales, the sperm whale has tiny eyes compared with those of most other mammals. But this does not matter because when the whale dives to feed, it descends deep into the ocean where light never reaches. It depends on its superb echo-location system to find its prey.

Did you know? Perfume is made from foul-smelling wax made in sperm whales' guts.

Did you know? A sperm whale can dive as deep as 3,000m in search of squid.

◀ LOOKING AROUND
A beluga raises its head above the water to look around – they are inquisitive creatures. Belugas have quite a short head with a rounded melon. Unusually for whales, it has a noticeable neck, allowing it to turn its head. It also has a wide range of facial expressions and often appears to be smiling.

◄ COW AND CALF
A sperm whale cow swims with her calf. Cows suckle their young for at least two years in a nursery group with other cows and calves. This picture shows the sperm whale's unique body shape, with its huge blunt snout. The sperm whale does not have a dorsal fin, just a triangular lump on its back.

► HIGH SOCIETY
This pod of belugas is swimming in Arctic waters off the coast of Canada. Belugas are usually found in such pods because they are very social animals. Note the typical body characteristics, including broad stubby flippers and the lack of a dorsal fin.

▼ LONG IN THE TOOTH
In freezing Arctic waters a male narwhal comes to the surface to blow, its long tusk raised. The tusk has a spiral shape and can be up to 3m long. It is one of the narwhal's two teeth. A small number of males produce twin tusks.

tusk

▲ COLOUR, SHAPE AND WEIGHT
The narwhal's stocky body is much like that of the beluga. Both grow up to about 5m long and weigh up to 1,500kg. The main difference is in the colour. Whereas the beluga is white, the narwhal is mostly a mottled dark and light grey.

Beaked, Pilot and Killer Whales

Beaked whales are named after their beak, which is rather like that of many kinds of dolphin. Unlike dolphins, they have hardly any teeth – most have just two. Beaked whales live mainly in the deep ocean, and little is known about them. Pilot and killer whales are better known. They are part of the dolphin family and, like many dolphins, tend to live in quite large groups. Because pilot whales and killer whales are mostly black, they are often called blackfish. The killer whale is the largest and best known of the family and is a fierce predator.

▲ **A TELLING TAIL**
A killer whale lob-tails. Its tail is black on top but mainly white underneath, with a distinct notch in the middle. Note also the pointed tips of the flukes.

Did you know? Killer whales have never been known to attack humans in the wild.

◀ **KILLER LEAP**
A killer whale leaps high into the air while breaching in Alaskan waters. The whale may twist and turn before it falls back to the surface with a resounding splash. Look at this killer whale's broad paddle-shaped flippers. The size and shape of the flippers and the dorsal fin mark this specimen as a male.

◄ CRUISING PILOT

The short-finned pilot whale has a broad, bulbous head, and is for this reason sometimes called the pothead whale. It has sickle-shaped flippers and a curved dorsal fin. This pilot whale prefers tropical and subtropical regions. The long-finned pilot whale is similar, but with slightly longer flippers, and lives in the Southern Hemisphere in both cool and warm waters.

► WHITE LIPS

A pod of melon-headed whales swim close together. One of them is spy-hopping, and shows its melon-shaped head. Note its white lips.

◄ SLEEK LINES

Note the streamlined body of the killer whale as it comes out of the water while performing at Sea World in California. The picture shows its white patches behind the eye and at the side, and the white chin. There is a greyish saddle patch behind the dorsal fin.

▼ FALSE TEETH

A false killer whale spy-hops. False killer whales have as many as 20 teeth in each jaw. It does not look much like the killer whale and is much smaller. It has no white patches and its head is more slender.

► LONER

A beaked whale swims alone. Most spend a lot of time alone or with one or two others. They prefer deep waters, and some species dive very deep indeed.

Oceanic Dolphins

Dolphins are the most common of all cetaceans. They are swift swimmers and have sleek, streamlined bodies with, usually, a prominent dorsal fin. They have dark grey backs and white or pale grey bellies. Many dolphins have contrasting stripes along the sides. About half the dolphin species have a long beak, and as many as 250 teeth. The rest have short beaks and fewer teeth. Dolphins can be found in most oceans, but not usually in the cold waters of far northern or far southern regions. Most are highly sociable, some travelling together in groups of hundreds.

◄ STRIKING STRIPES

Distinctive black and white striped bodies tell us that these two animals are southern right whale-dolphins. The back is jet black, while the beak, forehead, belly and flippers are white.

▼ PORPOISING DOLPHINS

A group of common dolphins is porpoising – taking long, low leaps. They have a long beak and yellow markings on their sides. The dark skin on the upper back looks rather like a saddle. This is why it is also called the saddleback dolphin.

Did you know? Dolphins make loud noises when hunting to panic fish into bunching together.

◀ GREAT LEAPERS

Two bottlenose dolphins launch themselves with great energy several metres into the air. Their bodies are mainly grey in colour. The head of the bottlenose dolphin is more rounded than that of most other beaked dolphins.

▶ BLUNT HEADS

A group of Risso's dolphins is easy to recognize by their blunt heads and tall dorsal fins. Their bodies are mainly grey on the back and sides. The colour becomes paler with age, and some old adults are nearly all white.

▼ PALE FACE

The odd-looking Irrawaddy dolphin has a rounded head and a distinct neck, rather like the beluga. Its flippers are large and curved. It is found in rivers and estuaries, as well as coastal waters from south of India as far as northern Australia.

Dolphin Rescue
An old Greek tale tells of a famed poet and musician named Arion. After a concert tour, sailors on the ship that was taking him home set out to kill him for his money. They granted his request to sing a final song. Then he jumped overboard. He did not drown because a dolphin, attracted by his beautiful song, carried him to the shore.

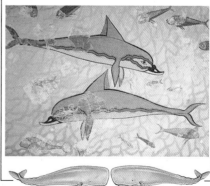

Porpoises and River Dolphins

Porpoises look rather like dolphins, yet they form a separate cetacean family. They are smaller than most dolphins and do not have a typical dolphin beak. Their teeth are different, being spade-like instead of cone-shaped. Most porpoises are shy. The rare river dolphins form a separate family. They have a long slender beak and a rounded forehead. Their flexible neck allows their head to turn, unlike oceanic dolphins. In the muddy waters where they mostly live, they use echo-location rather than their poor eyesight to find the fish and other creatures they feed on.

▲ BEAKED BOTO

The Amazon river dolphin, or boto, has the typical long beak of the river dolphins. Its colour varies from pale bluish-grey to pink. It has no dorsal fin, just a fleshy ridge on its back.

◄ RESTING PORPOISE

A Dall's porpoise displays the body features of its species. It has a stocky black body, with a large white patch on the sides and belly. Its dorsal fin and tail flukes have flashes of white as well. Unlike most porpoises, which are shy, the Dall's porpoise loves to bow-ride fast boats.

▼ RARE SNEEZER

Like all river dolphins, the Yangtze river dolphin, or baiji, has poor sight. Its blowhole is circular and its blow sounds like a sneeze! This dolphin is one of the rarest of all cetaceans, numbering maybe only 150 individuals.

Did you know? The harbour porpoises rarely seen in harbours.

▶ FAST AND FURIOUS

Dall's porpoises are the most energetic of all the porpoises. Their swimming is fast and furious. They kick up great fountains of spray as they thrust themselves through the surface of the water.

▶ NOISY SNORTER

The harbour porpoise seldom comes near boats. It has a noisy, snorting blow. The general body colour is dark grey on the back with paler patches on the flanks. Its belly is white, and it has black flippers and lips.

Did you know? Dall's porpoises are one of the fastest marine mamals – travelling up to 35 knots.

▼ DOLPHIN OR PORPOISE?

Porpoises are close relatives of dolphins, but they belong to a different family with different body features. Scientists can take advantage of strandings such as this one to study these very shy creatures.

Fellow Travellers

Whales are not the only aquatic mammals. Other examples include otters and seals. Seals are well adapted to life in the water, with a sleek, streamlined body and flippers. They have some fur, but it is the thick layer of fatty blubber under the skin that keeps them warm in the water. It also insulates against the cold air when seals are on land. The dugong and the manatee are also at home in the water. Often called sea cows, these creatures have a bulky seal-like body. They live in rivers and coastal waters in tropical and subtropical regions.

▲ BEAR AT SEA

The polar bear drifts on pack ice in the Arctic Ocean, often taking to the water to hunt seals. In addition to a thick layer of blubber, a polar bear has a thick furry coat to protect it from the Arctic climate.

◄ FIN-FOOTED

The Californian sea lion swims using powerful strokes of its front flippers. Its body is much more adapted to the water than an otter's, with its paddle-like flippers. Its body is partly hairy, partly smooth.

Did you know? Whales were probably descended from a 4-legged land mammal called a mesonychid.

► FURRY SWIMMER

The otter is at home on land or in water. Its four-legged, furry body is adapted for life in the water. Its legs are short, and its toes are webbed, making efficient paddles. Its fur is waterproof.

▲ WHALE-LIKE

The whale shark is not a whale, but the biggest fish of all – a harmless member of the shark family. The whale shark measures more than 15m long. It feeds on plankton, which it takes in through its gaping mouth. It sieves out the plankton from the water through a special gill structure.

Did you know? The largest whale shark ever caught weighed 15 tonnes.

◄ SEA COW

A dugong swims in the Pacific Ocean, just off Australia. Unlike the seals, which leave the water to breed on land, dugongs spend all their time in the sea. They have no hind limbs, but a tail, similar to that of a whale. The alternative name for the creature – sea cow – is a good one because the animal feeds on sea grasses.

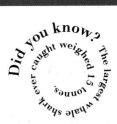

► EXCAVATOR

The walrus is a mammal of the seal family. Like the true seals, it has no external ears and it swims by means of its rear flippers. It feeds mainly on the seabed, using its whiskers to locate buried clams and its armoured snout to grub them out. The walrus excavates clams by squirting a high pressure jet of water from its mouth into the clam's burrow.

Whale Slaughter

The baleen whales and sperm whale are so big that they have no natural predators. Until a few hundred years ago, the oceans teemed with them. In the 15th and 16th centuries, whaling grew into a huge industry. Whales were killed for blubber, which could be rendered down into oils for candles and lamps. The industry expanded following the invention of an explosive harpoon gun in the 1860s, and by the 1930s nearly 50,000 whales a year were taken in Antarctica. In 1988, commercial whaling was banned.

▲ WHALE SOAP
The sperm whale was once a prime target for whalers. They were after the waxy spermaceti from the organ in the whale's forehead. This was used to make soap.

▶ DEADLY STRUGGLE
Whalers row out from a big ship to harpoon a whale in the early 1800s. It was a dangerous occupation in those days because the dying whales could easily smash the small boats to pieces.

Did you know? Whale blubber was made into lipstick and other sorts of make-up.

▼ FIN WHALING
A modern whaler finishes cutting up a fin whale. A few whales are still caught legally for scientific purposes, but their meat ends up on the table in some countries. The fin whale used to be a favourite target for whalers because of its huge size.

◀ PILOT MASSACRE
Every year in the Faroe
Islands of the North Atlantic
pods of pilot whales are
killed, a traditional practice
that has not been stopped.
The blood of the dying
whales turns the sea red.

Did you know? Early whalers killed their prey by throwing harpoons from rowing boats.

▶ KILLER NET
This striped
dolphin died when
it was caught in a
drift net. It
became entangled
and was unable to
rise to the surface
to breathe. Tens of
thousands of
dolphins drown
each year because
of nets cast into
the oceans.

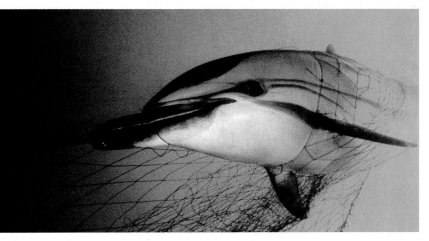

Did you know? In the 1800s baleen was used to make umbrellas.

'Whale Tale'
Moby Dick *was written by*
Herman Melville in 1851. The one-
legged Captain Ahab searches for a
great white whale (a sperm whale)
called Moby Dick. Eventually he
harpoons Moby Dick, but he and
all but one of his crew die.

THE SPERMACETI WHALE

Whale Conservation

If full-scale whaling had continued, many of the great whales would now be extinct. Even today, only a few thousand blue whales, right whales and bowhead whales remain. Because they are slow breeders, it will take a long time for numbers to recover. However the grey whale and the humpback whale appear to be recovering well. These two whales are favourites among whale-watchers because they are so approachable. Whale-watching has made people aware of what remarkable creatures whales are and why they must be protected.

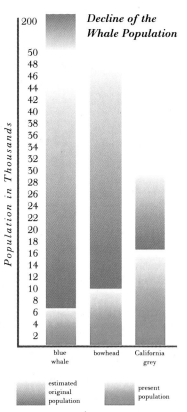

Population in Thousands

Decline of the Whale Population

200
50
48
46
44
42
40
38
36
34
32
30
28
26
24
22
20
18
16
14
12
10
8
6
4
2

blue whale   bowhead   California grey

estimated original population

present population

Did you know?
The first whale sanctuary was set up in 1946.

▲ GREY GREETING
A grey whale surfaces near a boat off the Pacific coast of Mexico. It is winter, and the greys have migrated to these warmer breeding grounds from the far north. Because these animals stay close to the shore, they are easy to reach by boat.

▲ WHALE RECOVERY
By the middle of the 20th century, the blue, bowhead and grey whales were close to extinction. Then whaling was banned. Now populations are recovering.

▼ HUMPBACK SPECTACULAR
A humpback whale breaches. It hurls its 30-tonne bulk into the air, belly up, and will soon crash back to the surface. Out of all the behaviour whale-watchers come to see, this is by far the most spectacular.

▶ FRIENDLY FLIPPER

One bottlenose dolphin character,
called Flipper, (played by several
dolphins), starred in a series of
TV programmes and films. These
focused attention on how intelligent
dolphins are, yet how vulnerable they are, too.

Did you know? You can adopt your own whale by contacting your own local whale and dolphin society.

◀ WHALE-WATCHING

A boatload of whale-watchers sees the
tail flukes of a humpback whale
disappear as the animal starts to dive.
The boat is cruising off the New
England coast of the United States
where some populations of humpbacks
feed during the summer months.

▶ PERFORMING KILLER

A killer whale leaps high out of the water
at a dolphinarium, drawing applause
from the huge crowd watching. In the
wild, the killer whale is a deadly
predator, but in captivity – with all
meals provided – it is docile and
friendly. However, the benefits
of keeping these creatures in
captivity are not certain.

Did you know? Some countries continue to hunt whales.

GLOSSARY

adaptation
A change in a living thing to suit a new set of conditions. This change helps the animal (or plant) to survive in its environment.

afterbirth
All the material which protects and sustains a baby in its mother's womb. This is pushed out of her body after the birth.

algae
A group of very simple plants, some of which are only the size of a single cell. Others, for example seaweed, are much larger. Most types of algae live in water, but they also grow on damp soil and tree trunks.

allomother
A female elephant that helps a mother elephant to give birth and to care for her young.

altitude
The height of a place given in metres (or feet) above sea level.

ambush
When an animal hides, waiting for prey to walk past, then pounces on it in a surprise attack.

ankus
A wooden pole ending in a metal point, usually with another hook set about 5cm back from the tip. It is used to prod working elephants in order to reinforce the commands given to them by their trainers.

Antarctic
The region around the South Pole and Southern Ocean, including the continent of Antarctica.

Arctic
The region of Earth around the North Pole.

artery
A blood vessel that carries blood away from the heart.

bacteria
A type of micro-organism – a living thing that cannot be seen by the naked eye. Huge numbers of bacteria live in the soil and break down dead material. Millions of bacteria live in the gut and on the skin of many animals, including humans.

baleen
A tough and flexible material, which forms comb-like plates in the upper jaw of baleen whales.

baleen whale
A whale that has baleen plates in its mouth instead of teeth.

beak
The protruding jaws of a whale or dolphin.

binocular vision
The ability to see things with both eyes at the same time. Binocular vision enables animals such as cats to judge distances and depths accurately.

bladder
Where waste urine is stored in the body before being expelled.

blow
The cloud of moist air that is blown from a whale's blowhole when it breathes out.

blowhole
The nostril of a whale. Baleen whales have two blowholes, toothed whales have one.

blubber
The layer of fatty tissue beneath the skin of a whale that acts as insulation against cold water.

bow-riding
The way whales and dolphins swim on the bow wave in front of a moving boat.

breaching
The way a whale leaps out of the water and falls back with a splash.

breed
An animal that belongs to one species, but has definite characteristics, such as colouring, body shape and coat markings.

bull
The adult male of certain species, such as whales and elephants.

bush elephant
The subspecies *Loxodonta africana africana*, which lives in the savanna grasslands of Africa.

calf
The baby of certain species, such as whales and elephants.

camouflage
Colours or patterns that allow an animal to blend in with its surroundings to avoid detection.

canine
A sharp, pointed tooth in carnivorous animals, used for killing and holding prey.

carnassial
A strong, shearing tooth at the back of a carnivore's mouth.

carnivore
An animal that feeds partly or mainly on the flesh of other animals.

cetacean
A whale, dolphin or porpoise, all of which belong to the animal order Cetacea.

classification
Arranging animals according to their similarities and differences in order to study them and suggest how they may be related.

conservation
Protecting living things and helping them to survive in the future.

continent
One of the seven main land masses on Earth. The continents are North America, South America, Europe, Africa, Asia, Australia and Antarctica.

cow
The name for an adult female of certain species, including whales and elephants.

crustacean
A creature with a hard body that lives in the sea. Shrimp and krill are crustaceans.

culling
Legally killing animals when there are too many to survive in one area. The idea is that culling some animals will leave more food and space for the remaining animals and help them to survive.

cultivation
The preparation and use of the ground in order to grow crops.

dentine
A hard substance, also called ivory, which makes up the bulk of the teeth of animals with backbones.

desert elephant
A possible subspecies of the African elephant, which lives in the deserts of Namibia.

dew claw
The digit (toe) on a cat's front foot that is held off the ground to keep it sharp. It is used to knock down and hold on to prey.

diet
The usual types of food eaten by an animal.

digestion
The process by which food is broken down so that it can be taken into the body.

DNA (deoxyribonucleic acid)
The genetic material inside the cells of most living organisms. It controls the characteristics that are passed on from parents to their offspring.

dolphin
A small, toothed whale that has cone-shaped teeth.

domestic cat
A species of cat whose wild ancestors were tamed by people and bred in captivity.

domestication
The process of bringing an animal under human control. Farm animals and pet cats and dogs have all been domesticated.

dominance
A system between social animals, such as lions, in which one or a few animals rule the group and have first choice over the other, more junior members.

dominant animal
A "top" animal that leads others of its own species and refuses to defer to any other member of its group.

dormant
When an animal lies motionless and inactive, as in sleep.

dorsal fin
The usually triangular fin on the back of a whale's body.

drought
A long period of dry weather when no rain falls.

echo-location
The method toothed whales use to find their prey. They send out pulses of high-pitched sounds and listen for the echoes produced when the pulses are reflected by objects in their path.

Elephas maximus
The latin name for an Asian elephant.

environment
The surroundings in which an animal or plant lives. It includes both living things (other animals and plants) and non-living things (such as stones, the air, temperature and sunlight).

Equator
An imaginary line running around the centre of the Earth, separating north from south.

estuary
The tidal mouth of a large river.

evolution
The continual process of gradual development is called evolution.

evolve
When an animal or plant species develops and changes over a long time. As conditions alter, living things change to become better adapted (suited) to surviving.

extinction
When a whole species or large group of animals or plants disappears, dying out completely.

fable
A story, often with a mystical theme, which is not based on fact.

fertilization
The joining together of a male sperm and a female egg to start a new life.

flipper
A whale's paddle-like forelimbs.

flukes
The tail of a whale.

fluking
When a whale raises its flukes into the air before diving.

forest elephant
The subspecies of African elephant, *Loxodonta africana cyclotis*, which is smaller than the bush elephant and lives in forests rather than grassland.

fossils
The preserved remains of living things, found in rocks.

genes
The material inside the cells of most living organisms. They control the characteristics passed on from parents to their offspring.

gland
An organ in the body that makes chemicals for a particular use.

grizzly bear
Another name for the brown bear. It is particularly used to mean North American brown bears.

habitat
A place that has certain kinds of animals and plants living there, such as tropical rainforest or semi-desert.

herbivore
An animal that eats plants.

herd
A large group of elephants, made up of several family units, together with groups of adult bulls. A large herd can consist of as many as 500-1,000 individual elephants.

hibernation
A period of sleep during the winter when body processes slow down. Animals hibernate mainly because food is scarce and they might starve otherwise.

Hinduism
One of the world's oldest religions, which began in India more than 5,000 years ago. Hindus worship several gods.

Ice Age
A time when large parts of the Earth were covered by glaciers and ice. The last Ice Age ended about 10,000 years ago.

ice floe
A sheet of ice floating in the sea.

incisor
Front tooth used for biting off chunks and cutting up meat.

infrasound
Very low sounds which are too low for people to hear.

insulation
A covering, such as the layer of thick fat beneath a polar bear's skin, that prevents heat leaving a warm body to the cold outside.

intestine
Part of an animal's gut where food is broken down and absorbed into the body.

Inuit
A people of the Arctic region, also known as Eskimos. The word Inuit, which means people, is preferred because Eskimo means eaters of raw meat and the Inuit cook at least part of their diet.

ivory
The dentine of teeth, usually that of tusks, such as those in elephants, walruses or narwhals.

jungle
The dense undergrowth found in a rainforest.

kidney
An organ in the body that filters blood to remove waste products, which are then expelled in urine.

krill
Tiny crustaceans that are the main source of food for many of the baleen whales.

liver
An organ that produces bile, which helps to process food from the digestive system (gut). One of the liver's main tasks is to remove any poisons from the blood.

lob-tailing
The way a whale raises its tail into the air and then slaps it down on the surface of the water.

Loxodonta africana cyclotis
The Latin name for an African elephant.

lung
An organ of the body that takes in oxygen from the air and removes carbon dioxide from the body.

Mahout
The Indian word for an elephant keeper, who tames and trains a working elephant.

mammal
A warm-blooded animal with fur or hair and a backbone, which can control its own body temperature. Female mammals feed their young on milk made in mammary glands (breasts) on their bodies.

mammoth
A large, woolly coated relative of the elephant that lived in cold places and died out about 10,000 years ago.

mangrove
Trees that grow in muddy swamps near the sea.

mastodon
Prehistoric elephants that lived in the woodlands of North America, but are now extinct.

mating
The pairing up of a male and female to produce young. During mating, fertilization of the female's egg takes place.

matriarch
In elephants, the experienced female that leads a family unit in the wild.

melon
The rounded forehead of a toothed whale. It is thought that the melon helps to direct the sounds the animal uses for echo-location.

membrane
A thin layer of skin that separates one area from another.

migration
A regular journey some animals make from one habitat to another, because of changes in the weather or their food supply, or in order to breed.

milk teeth
A young animal's first teeth, which are replaced by permanent teeth.

Moeritherium
A very early semi-aquatic elephant ancestor with only tiny traces of tusks and a trunk.

molar
A broad, ridged tooth in the back of a mammal's jaw, used for grinding up food.

muscle
An animal tissue made up of bundles of cells that can contract (shorten) to produce the body's movements.

musth
A period of aggressive, dangerous behaviour in bull elephants when they pick fights with other bulls and search for females that are ready to mate.

nerves
Fibres that carry electrical impulses to and from the brain.

nipple
A teat through which young suck milk from the mammary glands.

oesophagus
Part of a gut of an animal, usually long and tube-shaped. It transports swallowed food from the mouth to the stomach.

parasite
A living thing that lives on or in the body of another species, called its host, usually causing the host some harm.

pectoral fin
An alternative name for a whale's flipper.

pigment
Colouring matter.

plankton
Tiny sea creatures and plants. They form the basic foodstuff for all life in the oceans.

playfight
Early preparation for learning how to fight when cubs are older. Playing helps to build up muscles, improve co-ordination and develop good reflexes.

poaching
Capturing and/or killing animals illegally and selling them for commercial gain.

pod
A group of whales.

polar region
The area around the North or South Pole, where it is very cold.

porpoise
A small, toothed whale with spade-shaped teeth.

porpoising
When a porpoise leaps in and out of the water while swimming fast.

predator
A living thing that catches and kills other living things (prey) for food.

pregnant
When a female mammal has a baby developing in her womb.

prehensile tail
A tail that is capable of grasping and holding on to objects such as branches.

prehistoric
The period before people wrote down any historical records.

prey
An animal that is hunted for food by another animal (known as the predator).

rainforest
Dense forest that is hot and humid all year round. Rainforest is found in the regions of the world nearest to the Equator.

rodent
An animal with chisel-shaped incisors (front teeth) used for gnawing. Rats, mice, beavers and porcupines are all types of rodent.

rorqual
A baleen whale with grooves in its throat. The grooves allow the throat to expand when the animal is taking in water when it is feeding.

ruminant
An even-toed hoofed mammal (for example a cow or sheep), that chews the cud and has a stomach with four chambers.

savanna
Hot grassland with scattered trees that has wet and dry seasons.

scavenger
An animal that feeds mainly on the remains of a kill left behind by another animal.

school
Another name for a group of whales.

snorkle
A breathing tube a swimmer holds in their mouth so they can breathe while swimming just below the surface of the water.

social animal
An animal that lives in a group, usually with others of its own kind. Social animals co-operate with other group members.

species
A group of animals that share similar characteristics and can mate together to produce young.

splashguard
A raised area in front of the blowholes of some whales. It helps prevent water entering the blowholes when the whales breathe.

spout
Spout is another word for a whale's blow.

spy-hopping
The movement of a whale poking its head out of the water so that the eyes are above the surface.

Sri Lanka
Country off the coast of India.

stalk
To follow prey quietly and carefully so that a predator is within striking distance.

Stegadon ganesa
The most advanced of the prehistoric elephants in the mastodon group. *Stegadon ganesa* is believed to be a direct ancestor of the elephant.

stranding
Coming out of the water on to the shore and becoming stuck, or stranded.

streamline
The rounded, tapering shape that allows air or water to flow smoothly around an object.

subspecies
A species is sometimes divided into even smaller groups called subspecies, which are sufficiently distinct to have their own group.

suckle
Suck milk from the breast of a female mammal.

sweat glands
Small organs beneath an animal's skin that produce sweat. Sweat helps to keep the body cool.

tail fin
Another name for a whale's flukes.

taste buds
Tiny bumps on an animal's tongue, which have nerve endings that pick up taste signals.

temperate
Mild regions of the Earth that do not experience extreme heat or cold, wet or dry conditions.

territory
An area in which an animal or group of animals live. The borders of territories are marked, so that others of the same species know to keep out.

toothed whale
A whale that has teeth and not baleen plates in its mouth. Toothed whales include sperm whales, dolphins and porpoises.

trachea
The windpipe running from the nose and mouth to transport air to the lungs.

trail
A path through the forest or open ground that an animal such as a bear uses regularly.

tropical
The climate in the Tropics, the region on either side of the Equator, where the seas are always warm.

tundra
A treeless region of the Earth with permanently frozen soil just below the surface.

tush
The short tusk of an Asian or African elephant.

tusk
Long pointed tooth sticking out of an animal's mouth when it is closed.

vein
A blood vessel that carries blood back towards the heart.

warm-blooded
An animal that is able to maintain its body temperature at the same level all the time.

whale
A cetacean. Commonly the term is applied to the large whales, such as the baleen and sperm whales.

whalebone
A popular name for baleen, but baleen is not bone.

whaling
Hunting whales for their meat and blubber.

womb
An organ in the body of female mammals in which young grow and are nourished until birth.

INDEX

Conservation Addresses

African Wildlife Foundation
1717 Massachusetts Avenue,
NW Washington, DC 20036

American Bear Association
P.O. Box 77
Orr, Minnesota, USA
55771
Web site: http://www.americanbear.org/
E-mail: bears@vermilionnet.com

Bear Watch
1850 Commercial Drive
Box 21598
Vancouver, British Columbia, Canada
V5N 4AO
Web site: http://www.bearwatch.org
E-mail: bears@bearwatch.org

Born Free Foundation
Coldharbour
Dorking
Surrey
RH5 6HA

The Brown Bear Foundation
Isabel La Catolica. 7-4
39007 Santander, Cantabria, Spain
Web site: http://www.esegi.es/esegi/oso/texto/ihpage.html

International Union for the Conservation of Nature
Regional Office/ East Africa
PO Box 68200
Nairobi
Kenya

World Wildlife Fund (USA)
1250 Twenty-Fourth Street, NW
Washington, D.C., USA 20037
Web site: http:www.wwf.org